Praise for

Meeting in the Margins

"Cynthia Trenshaw is a gifted writer, massage therapist and pilgrim who has chosen to journey with those who are the most vulnerable in our society. As a writer, she conveys in vivid and powerful prose the heart-wrenching details of life on the street. As a massage therapist, she feels into their stories and anoints their soul-wounds with compassion and courage. As a pilgrim, she searches for meaning, her own and ours with every encounter. This is a prayer book as well as a textbook for those who choose to journey to the margins of society and be transformed."

—MARY ANN FINCH, founder/director of
Care Through Touch Institute and author of
Care Through Touch: Massage, the Art of Anointing

"*Meeting in the Margins* is a dangerous book. It will move you, shake you, change you, and leave you with a profound sense that you have been in the presence of the holy. Cynthia Trenshaw's intention is to do just that. She is a brilliant writer. Simply by telling the truth in stories that she herself has lived, she takes us into touching distance of those whom Rabindrinath Tagore called 'the poorest, the lowliest, and lost.' Profoundly trained in massage, in chaplaincy, in theology, Trenshaw ultimately lays all that down in the simplicity of touch. Touch as sacrament, touch as presence. In hospice, by the bedside of an AIDS victim, and in the Tenderloin district of San Francisco, she kneels (and so we kneel) and massages the feet, the body, the shoulders, the head of an "untouchable" (who has become ourselves). Doing so, she finds herself touched. And so does the reader. *Meeting in the Margins* is a powerful tool—it lifts us into hope; it belongs in the hands of all of those who would heal the broken world."

—PAT SCHNEIDER, author of *How the Light Gets In: Writing as a Spiritual Practice* and *Writing Alone and With Others*

"A beautifully written, challenging, and thought-provoking book, one that truly leads us to insights and recognitions that make it possible to contemplate a world that works for all. I haven't seen anything like it. Cynthia's book contributes to helping us see the world at the margins with clarity."

—MARGARET J. WHEATLEY, founder of the Berkana Institute and author of *So Far From Home, Perseverance, Turning to One Another,* and *Leadership and the New Science*

"Cynthia Trenshaw gifts us with an extraordinary window into the soul of the marginalized among us. In exquisite detail of both inner and outer moments of meeting on the streets, the reality of presence she evokes communicates through her stories; it sparks our own celebration of that precious sense of presence. Prepare to be deeply touched. Prepare to remember what is truly important in our lives. This book is itself a gift from soul to soul. Through her open-hearted memories, Trenshaw offers us all a most generous and luxurious soul massage!"

—RABBI TED FALCON, PHD author of *A Journey of Awakening* and co-author of *Religion Gone Astray* and *Getting to the Heart of Interfaith*

"Cynthia Trenshaw has nerves of steel and a heart of gold, and she does a superb job of taking readers along with her as she carefully tends to some of the most overlooked and down-trodden members of our society. She steadfastly shines the light of compassion upon the lives of individuals who have fallen by the wayside in our fast-paced mainstream culture, showing readers that underneath the often shabby appearance of each of these individuals lies something else quite unexpected: tenderness, humor, wisdom, even a certain kind of nobility. I recommend her book to all readers who are not afraid to step outside their usual comfort zone and have an eye-opening, heartwarming experience amidst misfits and castoffs."

—BETSY MACGREGOR, MD, co-founder of the Enso House Residence for Care at the End of Life and author of *In Awe of Being Human: A Doctor's Stories from the Edge of Life*

Meeting
in the
Margins

Earlier versions of three chapters from *Meeting in the Margins* have been published elsewhere; "Jabberwocky," in *Soundings Review*, Spring 2010, published by the Northwest Institute of Literary Arts; "Sheltered Woman" and "Mack the Hermit" in *Pain and Memory: Reflections on the Strength of the Human Spirit in Suffering* (Editions Bibliotekos, Inc., 2009).

Published 2015
Printed in the United States of America
ISBN: 978-1-63152-816-3
Library of Congress Control Number: 2015936840

Book design by Stacey Aaronson

For information, address:
She Writes Press
1563 Solano Ave #546
Berkeley, CA 94707

She Writes Press is a division of SparkPoint Studio, LLC.

Meeting in the Margins:

An Invitation to
Encounter Society's Invisible People

❧

by
Cynthia Trenshaw

SHE WRITES PRESS

This book is dedicated,
with love and admiration,
to the people I meet in the margins
who continue to teach me.

ACKNOWLEDGMENTS

I am so grateful to the women of the Grand Rapids Dominican Congregation, who have believed in me, prayed for me, supported me with a graduate scholarship, and bolstered me spiritually in every margin into which I have ventured; and to Christina, Marian, Margaret, and all the other midwives who had a hand in bringing this book to birth.

CONTENTS

FOREWORD

hearsay (hear · say)

*1. unofficial information gained or acquired from
another and not part of one's direct knowledge or
experience*

We pass them by. On city streets while we hurry to work or
lunch or an evening's entertainment; on the curbs of small
towns waiting for Walmart to open, stumbling out of
shelters while we thread our way around them. Us; them.
Not sure what to do, we tend to avert our gaze, step
around, step over, cross the street, tighten our hold on
wallets, purses, and briefcases, pull a coat closer around our
shoulders. Boundary. Barrier. We are on the good side of
fortune and want to stay here, don't want our trajectories
soiled by interaction with those who have fallen off the
path of a reasonable life.

They watch us pass by. They search for our gaze, for a
sign of recognition, for some small signal of acknowledg-
ment that we are brushing through shared space. Them; us.
Not sure what else to do, they tighten their hold on begging
cups, rangy dogs, sickly children, drunken comrades,
shopping carts, and lumpy bundles. Boundary. Barrier.
They are on the losing side of fortune and see us from the
other side of a chasm they have forgotten how to clamber
back across.

Who are they? We don't know.

Who are we? They don't know.

Why should we know?

Are our minds open enough to consider the possibility that our view of the world would be enriched by expanding the boundaries of who we see?

What if we risked curiosity and compassion?

We are, after all, sharing time and space with one another on life's perilous journeys.

The challenge of this book is to say *yes*, to open our minds and to follow Cynthia Trenshaw's open heart. She dares to cross the chasm and bring us back stories that introduce us.

Do we dare to read and be moved by what she knows?

People are storytelling/storycatching creatures: this is our niche. We fill the world with words. We are the only creatures who can be moved to action by the power of words alone. We come to love or hate, to include or exclude, to make peace or make war on the power of hearsay. We take each other's word for reality. We seek stories to explain events and we pass them on. Storytelling and storycatching is a compulsive neurological behavior. The brain fills in gaps of knowledge with story; if we don't have facts, we fabricate coherence. We are compelled to create narrative, to explain to ourselves what is going on. The true gift of this book is that Cynthia is harvesting stories of her experiences with marginalized people. She is bringing us coherence so that we may be moved to fill in the gaps between us and react differently with those we pass by.

Words are how we think; story is how we link. Story gives us a neurological pathway to connect one human experience to another by seeking common elements that emerge in very different situations. I identify with the dedi-

cation of a homeless woman to her dog because of my own dedication to my dog. I see the struggle of a man to make a "home" for the night in a doorway because I recognize my own desire to come to rest at the end of the day in a self-designed sphere of safety.

Narrative linkage is the source of our human capacity to learn vicariously, to absorb experiences we have not actually had and integrate them into our knowledge base. Through this storycatching capacity we can have a broader view of the world than we have through actual experience. Vicarious learning is one of the great, universal skills of the human being. We story each other into knowledge, into wisdom, into a greater chance at survival.

Cynthia Trenshaw crosses into the margins to meet our society's invisible people: the hospitalized and the dying, the mentally and physically and addictively ill, the homeless, and the people of the streets. She offers us what she learns—what they tell her, what they want us to know. Now we have the opportunity to read and be changed by her unflinching and compassionate prose.

Through the stories in this book, we go places that we might not have the courage or opportunity to go to in our day-to-day reality. The world becomes a bigger, more complex, more interesting place. When the author's friend, Chris, comes from Michigan to visit San Francisco, Cynthia teaches her to see the folks at the margins, and invites her to come along and offer simple hand massage to street people under the auspices of The Care Through Touch Institute. We readers are invited to join Chris in this transformational experience.

Reading, I go through my own fear, my own revulsion.

Reading, I eventually I find my willingness to ride the shoulders of this story into vicarious experience.

After reading the book, I find myself behaving differently on downtown streets. I find that reading has changed my sight and my insight. I notice the marginalized folks around me. I notice that I am not so avoidant of them. I notice that I have learned some street smarts from Cynthia's stories. I have come prepared. I have ten one-dollar bills folded separately in my coat pocket. If I feel the impulse to give in response to being asked, I'm ready. I don't have to dig in my purse. I have four power bars in my other pocket, something nutritious as well as sweet.

Reading has given me access to my own empowerment. I walk the city streets able to pass my fellow human beings with open eyes. I see the boundary, the barrier, and I create tiny moments when I carefully reach across it with a smile, a sentence of acknowledgment, or one of my pocketed gifts. I am not a social worker or case manager. I am not a massage therapist. I am not a caretaker or guardian. I am a passerby; they are passersby. I may not know their particular story, but I know they carry one. And maybe I will have the courage to pause long enough to listen, to say, "You take care of yourself, now . . . hear?"

Thank you, Cynthia, for showing me, and the many readers of this book, the doorway into "us."

—Christina Baldwin

Author of *Storycatcher: Making Sense of our Lives through the Power and Practice of Story*

*F*or twenty years my workplaces have been one city's infamous slums, and another city's hospital corridors and emergency room cubicles. I've served in nursing homes, hospices, and the home bedrooms of the dying.

I have sought out people who live in the margins of our culture. Invisible people. Not socially "worthy" people or people who are prepared to change their lives, but people who allow me simply to be with them and perhaps to touch them.

I have gone to the margins as a massage therapist, as a chaplain, and as a bedside caregiver. I shall never know whether my presence has changed anyone else's life. But their receptivity to me, and the life lessons they have offered by their own presence, have certainly transformed me.

By entering into the margins of our culture, my physical senses were altered to become the agents of my heart. My heart learned to recognize what my senses had long been programmed to reject.

My ordinary eyes were transformed into "marginal eyes," able to see in the cultural darkness. And so I was gifted with exquisite human teachings I would otherwise have missed.

As you enter this book, I invite you to allow your perceptions to be changed. I invite your ordinary eyes to become marginal eyes, able to see marginalized people, the socially invisible, our banished kin.

I invite your heart to hear what they have to teach us.

PROLOGUE

GLORIA – AN ENCOUNTER
Spring 2001

*S*he looked like a used-up prostitute. Probably she was. Her forty-some years had been hard ones. She had skin the color and texture of old dried figs.

She sat on a bench, arms crossed, head down, folded into herself. She and I were two of dozens of people in the park—a long stretch of concrete and trees in the middle of downtown San Francisco. The sun was warm and the breeze was mid-March mild, but she wore a red velvet winter coat with a white fake-fur collar. Her purple lipstick was smeared across her left cheek and onto the fuzzy left lapel. Exhausted, or drunk, or high, or some combination of the three, she studied my approach with her eyelids hovering at half-mast.

It was Maundy Thursday, when the Christian calendar commemorates a day when Jesus knelt to wash the feet of his friends. Several of us massage therapists went out this day to offer foot massages to homeless people on the streets of downtown San Francisco.

I introduced myself to her and made my offer. She said her name was Gloria. Her eyes asked, *what's the catch here? Do you really know what you're asking?* Nevertheless, she removed her battered red high-heeled shoes. Then she hesitated, in unaccustomed embarrassment at revealing a part of her body that others seldom saw. Finally she rolled down

her knee-high stockings, damaged with snags and runs almost past redemption, and pulled them off.

I sit on the ground before her, put my backpack between us, and drape a clean towel over it. I prop her bared feet on the makeshift ottoman. I spread antibacterial gel over my palms and work it into my fingers, showing her that I am concerned for her well-being.

Then I smooth massage lotion between my palms, slowly—no rush, we have all the time we need for this—taking the chill off the lotion with the warmth of my hands before I touch her feet.

My hands curve around her right ankle to raise her foot; I cup her heel in my left palm and place my right hand over her arch. No need to do anything else, just hold this dark, callused foot of this unknown woman, just hold it, just breathe into the moment. There is nowhere else to be but this place where my skin touches her skin, no time but this time when her feet have brought her to this park and my hands have offered this work. Our shared connection at her foot becomes a bridge across which her stories and mine now begin wordlessly to cross.

As my fingers stroke lotion over her foot, her skin hears the silent story of the therapeutic skills I've learned for her.

As I trace the bones of her misshapen foot, my thumbs listen to her mute memoir. Her feet are dirty, her toes deformed; fungus grows under her nails. Chunks of dirt and slough fall from wherever I touch. It does not matter, because beneath my fingers I can feel a softening in her tired and neglected feet.

The kindness and pleasure she receives now are

echoing back from her feet to my hands; I am lost in the return of that same kindness and pleasure. The feet I am massaging have become my own feet, and I can feel the strength of my thumbs kneading at the base of my own toes. This woman whom I touch has mysteriously become me; her journey has become mine.

Gloria didn't speak during the twenty minutes that I worked. When I had brought the massage to completion, I sat, silent and still, looking up to study Gloria's face. It took several minutes for her to be aware that my hands had left her feet and for her to come back from the timeless space she had entered. Slowly her eyelids rose. She looked me straight in the eyes, and the intensity of her gaze would not allow mine to stray from hers. She said, clearly and thoughtfully, "This isn't just about massage, is it."

It was a statement, not a question, and not at all what I expected. It unsettled me. But she had more to say in her rhythmic, challenging statement/questions.

"This is about receiving, isn't it." A pause.

"And this is about giving, isn't it." A longer pause.

"And . . . "—she searched for the right word—"and . . . it's reciprocal, isn't it."

She focused on me long enough to make sure I'd heard her. Then she nodded once, satisfied, and her eyes closed again. But my mouth hung open. For, with my butt on the city pavement, with Gloria's sole-skin and accumulated dirt all over my hands, with my heart glowing from the soul work we had exchanged, I had just heard a homeless prostitute proclaim what had taken me years to understand.

It's reciprocal.

PART ONE:

Six Lessons

No questioning, no analysis, no distinctions—
just bearing witness to what's present.
The less we sort, judge, categorize or distinguish,
the more we see and feel.
—Margaret Wheatley, *Perseverance*

I

INITIATION

August 1996

The Berkeley trattoria hummed with animated conversations. On my plate a few strands of fettuccini still swam languidly in garlic and cream. The globe of thin glass in my hand had been filled for the third time, and I smiled at the candle flame distorted through the satiny red wine. We were anticipating what Mary Ann promised was "the best tiramisu in the Bay Area."

And I had just made the suggestion that would alter the trajectory of my life for the foreseeable future. I had said, in utter naivety, "Why don't I come with you one day? If I see what you do out there and get a closer look at the street people, I'll have better examples for the grant proposals."

Woody Allen once remarked, "If you want to hear God laugh, tell Him about your plans."

I was a middle-aged widow, recently arrived in Berkeley to study for a post-graduate degree in theology. My plan

was that in two years I would return to my Michigan home, degree in hand, to claim a position as chaplain for Hospice of Greater Grand Rapids.

But at the moment I was renewing my friendship with Mary Ann Finch, founder of the Care Through Touch Institute, who had taught my basic massage therapy certification course a year and a half earlier. Since I was back in Berkeley, I planned to give her a few hours of my time raising money for the Institute. Mary Ann was pioneering a new program in San Francisco, taking massage therapy literally to the streets and to the homeless people who lived there. She was so focused on the destitute people she served that she gave almost no attention to herself or to any fundraising, even for her own salary. She was, ironically, courting the danger of becoming homeless herself. I'd spent a few years as a grant writer, so I could offer her those skills, at least until I went back to Michigan—as planned.

And God was laughing, because, regardless of what I planned, the Midwest would never again be my home. I'd never again serve as a chaplain. I'd not serve in a hospice until ten years down the road. I was in free-fall into the second half of my life. So recently had I stepped off the edge of that particular cliff, and so unaware was I of the step, I hadn't yet felt even my first surge of vertigo.

I had no clue that I would soon be navigating a new and complex path of fear and compassion. Before long I'd be taking in unbearable sights and smells. I'd be emulating Mary Ann's fierce protectiveness of destitute men and women. Within weeks I'd begin connecting skin-to-skin with the untouchable people of the streets. Even as we finished our elegant dinner, "normal" for me was morphing

wildly into a landscape of wounded, hungry humans exiled to the shadows and crevices—the margins—of the San Francisco I thought I knew.

"How about Wednesday morning?" Mary Ann asked. She smiled innocently, though she must have known how fateful this moment's decision was. Surely she knew.

I might have noticed some challenge in her eyes, but the tiramisu arrived just then, and I said, "Sure," as the first forkful of impossibly delicate mascarpone cheese, sponge cake, and coffee liqueur wrapped itself around every taste bud in my mouth. After that there was no room in my head for anything else. Certainly there was no room for warning bells.

<center>❧</center>

Crossing the Threshold

Just sixty hours later, Wednesday morning arrives, and I feel a vague sense of volunteer's remorse. I've never been to the slums of San Francisco, so I can't fully imagine how horrible they might be, let alone how scary the people who inhabit their recesses. What was I thinking the other night? Why did I agree to this? And when, exactly, did I agree to it? Can I still back out?

Okay, I tell myself, I'll go, but I'll watch, take notes while Mary Ann works, then hightail it back across the Bay Bridge before nightfall.

The reader may insert God's chuckle here. Or she may insert religious historian Mircea Eliade's words about initiation: "In order to be created anew, the old world must first be annihilated."

I climb into Mary Ann's old tan battleship of a car with its petite owner behind the wheel. She is wearing her usual garb for Care Through Touch work: a colorful skirt and sweater, dangly earrings, sturdy shoes, a bracelet or two; her red backpack is tossed in the back seat, along with boxes of dis-infectant gel, small bars of soap, some folded blankets, and lots of pairs of new socks.

She skillfully navigates the streets of Berkeley, the Bay Bridge, and the traffic of San Francisco, and pulls into a public parking lot at Golden Gate Avenue and Jones Street. While she pays the parking fee, I look around, beyond the chain-link fencing that encloses the lot. Gray people sit on the sidewalk, leaning back against the fence. Gray people walk, carrying plastic bags or pushing broken grocery carts. Gray people lie sleeping on the sidewalk across the street. We are in the Tenderloin, a twenty-block triangle of concen-trated deprivation, grime, and human suffering. Not a docu-mentary, not a four-page spread in a news magazine—this is the real thing. My thoughts short out as I try to reconcile this reality with my presence in it. How has this happened? And how soon can I leave?

We begin to walk down Jones Street, with Mary Ann stopping every few yards to squat down and talk to someone, or to greet people who call out her name. I follow her progress down the sidewalk, but her actions now seem muddled. Nothing here is familiar to me. There is nothing comfortable, nothing clean, nothing organized, nothing I can relate to. Windows are broken or boarded up. Urine, spilled coffee, and cheap wine make tiny varicolored streamlets across the sidewalks. Trash bins are bashed in. Even the parking meters are broken, their looted heads lolling at odd angles. Out of

the corner of my eye I notice that a pile of trash moves a bit, and I don't know whether it contains a person, or rodents, or both. No one seems "normal" here, not even Mary Ann. I wish fervently that I could just hide deep in the safety of her backpack. I want to close my eyes, but fear that I'd trip over someone if I did. My face feels numb from tension, and terror is suffocating me. Have I been pulled into some extra-terrestrial ritual for which, at any moment now, I'll be offered as the unwitting sacrifice?

Eventually we make our way to one of the many SRO (single room occupancy) hotels in the Tenderloin. We climb up three flights of dingy stairs, and walk down a narrow, ill-lit hallway. Mary Ann knocks on the door marked 307, and we enter Marjorie's world. It is, as advertised, a single room, maybe twelve feet square. It is occupied by the widest variety of sizes, colors, and speeds of cockroaches that I've ever seen. It is also occupied by Marjorie, whose knee was injured, she says vaguely, "by shrapnel in Vietnam."

Mary Ann introduces us, and after a few phony-feeling pleasantries, I lean cautiously against a sticky wall to watch. Marjorie sits on the edge of her bed and rolls up her pant leg. Mary Ann perches on an overturned milk crate with Marjorie's bared knee positioned across her lap. Her delicate hands touch and trace the scars while she talks to Marjorie, her voice as gentle as her strokes. I have finally relaxed enough to remember to take my notepad and pen from my pocket when I hear, "Cynthia, why don't you come over here and see what you think about this?"

I am not conscious of leaving my place against the wall, or of bending to sit down where Mary Ann was a moment before. But this is definitely me, perched on the plastic crate with a

*homeless woman's pain-filled leg draped across my lap. These
are definitely my fingers palpating the damaged tissue in her
knee. My conscious understanding of massage therapy and
anatomy has fled the room, but so, somehow, has my terror.*

*I have no verbal assessment for Mary Ann, but no doubt
she recognizes in my face and my posture that something has
changed. My hands seem to have minds of their own; I am a
bemused stranger whose rational brain is napping as my
fingertips tenderly seek, through Marjorie's knee, any resource
of healing within her, anything that could be called forth to
ease her pain.*

*Marjorie sighs, and the tension in her leg relaxes. I
murmur something to her, I think; maybe I only breathe quietly
for a few more minutes before slowly drawing my hands
away. She does not know I am no longer holding her knee;
her body is doing its own work for her.*

*I came here as a grant writer. I agreed only to watch Mary
Ann at her work; I wanted to "see the street people" she
worked with. There was no mention of my doing anything, least
of all touching anyone. How is it possible, then, that I have just
been initiated into the work of bringing caring touch to the
people of the streets?*

~

THE ELEMENTS OF RITUAL, TENDERLOIN-STYLE

In his 1958 book *The Rites and Symbols of Initiation*, Mircea
Eliade wrote: "Initiation is equivalent to a basic change in
existential condition; the novice emerges from his ordeal
endowed with a totally different being from that which he
possessed before his initiation; he has become another."

I had bought the 1994 paperback reprint of Eliade's book as a resource for a college paper on the symbolism of initiation. I had dog-eared a couple of pages, then promptly forgotten about the book when my paper was done. But the concepts would come powerfully rushing back to me later, on the day in which I underwent my own initiation into the particular "ordeal" called the Tenderloin.

The moment I stepped out of Mary Ann's car into the Tenderloin parking lot that day, I left behind everything that was familiar to me. Though I wanted to retreat to the known and the safe, I had already crossed an invisible line. I had done something that could not be undone. The self who had approached that line had faded away, and a new self was already confronting the unknown, putting one reluctant foot in front of the other, propelling herself to her future.

The time in Marjorie's room had more components of a religious ritual than I could have realized at the time. The minute I entered the room, the unfamiliar ambience took my breath away; my body responded with awe, as it might have done in a European cathedral just before Mass. But here, instead of embroidered Belgian linen altar cloths, were filthy bed sheets. Instead of acolytes there were scurrying cockroaches; instead of candles, a single bare light bulb; instead of incense, body odors; instead of vestments, Mary Ann's bright skirt. Mary Ann's voice, using ordinary comforting words, was nevertheless that of a priestess intoning sacramental rubric, and her hands moved with the surety of sacred gestures become intrinsic from years of use.

And then the priestess invited me to the altar, invited

me to position myself to partake of the sacrament: "Cynthia, why don't you come . . ."

Take and touch, this is the Body . . .

In the same way that a Christian may not have words for the significance of the Eucharist but intuits it, so I understood instinctively that Marjorie and I had merged with the Divine in the places where my flesh touched hers. I knew that the exchange between my proffered hands and her damaged knee had wakened something healing in her, and I realized that the same exchange had allowed something vital to enter my life.

A century ago, French anthropologist Arnold van Gennep identified three phases of initiation: separation, transition, and reincorporation. His research was conducted among pre-modern peoples, but the categories apply to events in our modern society as well. They apply to rites of passage of any size, whether a baby's circumcision, a girl's reception into a Brownie troop, a wedding, a two-week spiritual retreat, or even being born. We leave our former state, enter a place of mystical change, and return to the place we left as same-but-different people who must figure out whether and how we still belong there.

Often a well-thought-out intention precedes an initiation: a girl longs to become a Scout and cajoles her mother into becoming a troop leader; an adult craves a spiritual experience on a vision quest, seeks a guide, and follows the preparation instructions; a couple declare themselves engaged, apply for a marriage license, and create a ceremony to proclaim their growing love in the presence of their community.

Or the intention may be set by others on behalf of the

initiate: a Jewish baby has not asked for a bris, no one remembers asking to be born, and I had had no intention of spending a good portion of the next five years of my life among destitute people on the streets of San Francisco.

Sometimes it happens that the intention part of initiation is bypassed altogether. You are separated from your former life and hurled into the transition phase with no conscious preparation or forethought. There may be illness or an accident; there may be divorce or unemployment that you didn't see coming. There are crimes and climate changes and acts of God. And there is God's sense of humor. But always there are the three phases—separation, transition, reincorporation—held together by an explicit or implicit sense of the sacred and the mystical.·

The word *mystical* comes from a Greek word meaning "an initiate." *Mystical* means "inspiring a sense of spiritual mystery, awe, and fascination." And that sums up my first mystical time in the Tenderloin: the huge mystery of how I came to be in that area of San Francisco, of how I came to be in that room, touching that body. There was mystery in how awe began replacing my dread, filling up the entire space carved into my interior by fear just moments before. And there was mystery in the fascination—a fascination that I feel even today as I write these words—a mixture of curiosity, delight, and hunger for more.

❧

Return

As we retrace our steps back to the car, the journey for me could not be more different from the one just an hour before.

Now I feel I belong here. Rather than recoiling and re-treating, I open my mind and my heart to the people I pass. I make eye contact, say a few words in greeting. God help me, I actually touch a few hands and am reluctant to leave. I want to come back to this place and these people. I am impossibly, illogically in love with the streets and with the people for whom they are home. I have a lot yet to learn about how to work and be safe on the streets. I will need a lot of experience to hone the skills unique to street massage. But I am bubbling over with enthusiasm. I can't wait to tell my classmates where I've been today. . . . Oh, my classmates! My professors! How will I tell them, make them understand? Whatever will they make of this . . . this . . . whatever has happened to me. Have I lost my mind?

Probably.

Wonderful!

❧

In 1958 Mircea Eliade wrote that experiences of initiation "lead us into a world that cannot be described, but only 'narrated,' for it consists in the history of acts freely undertaken, of unforeseeable decisions, of fabulous transformations." Eliade knew how difficult it would be to explain the "initiation" that happened to me that day four decades later in 1996, how impossible to find the words. Most of my classmates and teachers eventually understood, or at least accepted, my enthusiastic reports. And yes, many thought I had lost my mind. During the next year, however, some would choose to join me in working on the streets.

Touch

*T*oday, I understand that my call to initiation in the Tenderloin really began nearly three years earlier, in February 1994. That was when I felt a first subtle itch to learn intentional touch. I was working as a hospital chaplain, too busy to pay much attention to this new yearning; I worried at it absently for several months, not certain what to call it, not certain it was even really there. But clarity came one day when I was visiting with an AIDS patient named Charlie.

The large signs on the door to Charlie's room instructed anyone who entered to put on a gown and mask, to scrub his or her hands thoroughly upon coming and leaving, and to wear disposable gloves.

I hated wearing the mask. So much of communication depends on being able to read a face—and sometimes I broke the hospital's protocol and lowered my mask after I was in Charlie's room. I also pinned my name badge on the outside of the gown, to silently re-offer my name to him.

He was in a single-bed room, isolated at the far end of the hallway. The AIDS epidemic was at its height in the United States; forty thousand Americans would die of the disease that year, and Charlie would be one of them. He had purple lesions on his face that clashed cruelly with his

brilliant blue eyes and his inquisitive brows. He had pneumonia, and his compromised lungs turned his words into strained whispers.

Charlie knew he was dying, and it was a relief to him to be able to speak about it. Too many friends and even professionals didn't want to discuss his dying; some tried to assure him he'd soon get better. But Charlie knew the truth, and I was willing to hold that truth with him. He could explore his own thoughts with me and express his emotions if he chose.

My memories of all my times with Charlie coalesce now into one day—the day in which my touching him taught me what I had to do next.

In this memory I am sitting in a folding chair pulled up parallel to the side of his bed. I don't recall the conversation; we may have been speculating on what death feels like. As I often did, I held his right hand in mine, our thumbs wrapped around each other. My left hand rested comfortably on his right shoulder. Many who came to this room wouldn't touch Charlie (except as a clinical necessity), though he hungered for the comfort that human touch can bring. Like parched, exhausted soil he soaked up compassionate touch, and that is how Charlie taught me: in a moment of thoughtful silence between us, with my hands on his arm, I experienced a corresponding thirst of my own, a frisson of need running between my two hands, up my arms, across my heart. It was an ache, a longing to know how to touch Charlie in a healing way. "Healing" wasn't even the right word, for I knew that Charlie would soon die. But I desperately wanted for my hands to learn something indefinably "more," and to offer it to Charlie.

My yearning had become manifest, and for the first time this thought crossed my mind: "I want to learn massage therapy."

A few weeks later a friend and I were at lunch, and one of us (I can't remember which) mentioned massage. Each, unbeknownst to the other, was thinking of taking massage training. My friend mentioned a course she'd read about in a magazine: a 180-hour, month-long program offered by the Care Through Touch Institute based in Berkeley, California. The training led to state certification as a massage practitioner. It was called Massage as the Art of Anointing, a unique spirituality-based massage therapy course. The title sent a responding thrill through me. I worked in a Catholic hospital, and anointing has long been recognized as a means of grace in Catholicism.

My mind raced ahead, rehearsing the religious rationale, imagining me getting permission from my supervisor, a nun, to take a month's leave-of-absence for a training that would add the sacramental of healing touch to my repertoire as a chaplain. My friend and I began talking about going together to Berkeley.

In the end my friend chose to be trained locally, but I got my leave-of-absence and flew to California for my training in January of 1995.

TOUCH AS SCIENCE

The course was held at the Graduate Theological Union (GTU), a consortium of nine theological seminaries: Baptist, Episcopal, Lutheran, Presbyterian, Dominican, Franciscan, Jesuit, Unitarian, and interdenominational, plus

Greek Orthodox, Judaic, and Buddhist Institutes. This campus, described in the promotional literature as "the place where religion meets the world," is situated on Berkeley's "holy hill," just north of the University of California campus. Many of those registered for the massage therapy training were already on sabbatical at GTU or were taking courses at one of the GTU seminaries, and so had their own apartments. The rest of us were housed for the month in a variety of places nearby.

Another student and I shared a guest room in a Benedictine priory where, on my first morning there, it took my Midwestern sensibilities a while to figure out just where I was. From my journal of that time:

> *January 3, 1995. They tell me I'm in California, though it's difficult for me to believe. There are traffic sounds outside and some people sounds, just like Grand Rapids—could be just about anywhere. But there is also the sound of a fountain in the small courtyard below, flowing not frozen. And there are bamboo and eucalyptus growing outside my window, and camellia blossoms in January. And directly below my room there is the sound of a dozen male Benedictine voices chanting morning prayer. Perhaps we're not in Michigan after all, Toto.*

It's embarrassing to admit it, but somehow I hadn't expected to have to study in order to become a massage practitioner. I guess I thought the training faculty would say "rub the arm this way" and "hold the foot like this." Maybe there would be a few techniques for applying oil to skin. But physiology? Anatomy? Specific massage sequences?

Wait a minute! Sure, they were basic-level courses and taught in a way that made learning fun, but still, at the end of the basics and the clever mnemonics, all that information had to be absorbed and regurgitated in a battery of genuine tests. Furthermore, it had to become embodied because there was the nervous-making final practical exam: giving a full-body massage to one of the Care Through Touch Institute faculty.

We learned *petrissage* (applied pressure and kneading to compress underlying muscles), *effleurage* (a soothing, stroking movement), *tapotement* (a rhythmic percussion with the tips of the fingers), and friction (strokes perpendicular to the muscle fibers). In the first two days we learned the muscles of the back, the buttocks, and the back of the leg. We exchanged back-massage work with classmates, and I was delighted to discover that the giver enjoys a massage almost as much as the receiver.

On January 6, just the third day of our training, we began studying the major joints of the body and their connective tissues. To more fully understand joints, fascia and connective tissue, we dissected chicken legs and thighs. That afternoon we set up a dozen massage tables around the room, and were ready to learn the sequences for massaging the legs and buttocks. My journal tells me that Carl and I worked together, and it was NOT a great experience. He was tense and had lots of stuff wrong with his legs and feet; he got leg cramps as I was working on him. I was trying to tend to his needs and at the same time follow the instructions that the rest of the class was hearing. I could not get centered, never did get a rhythm going with

my own body. It was generally a dissatisfying experience. When it was his turn to be the giver his work on me was tentative and fearful, and it was difficult for me to relax.

I was too new to this work to understand how much I learned from Carl that afternoon, even though it felt at the time like a mutually "failed" experience. This was my first lesson in how important intention is in massage. It was the first time I recognized how the therapist has to set aside her own concerns in order to focus solely on the receiver. I would later learn how to stay with a client at whatever stage they are in the moment, and not impose my own agenda for how they "should" progress. I would learn that if there is any healing possible, I can encourage it, but it will happen on its own schedule, not mine.

TOUCH AS SACRAMENT

Our training was richly holistic, involving not just mind and hands and massage sequences, but also heart and spirit and creativity. The day I worked with Carl happened to be Epiphany, when the Western Christian calendar remembers the dreams and the journey and the gifts of the Magi. Our morning physical warm-up exercises had included a "dream reach" sequence of yoga and "the pilgrim's walk" (three steps forward and one step back). At the end of the day, we were asked to put away the massage tables and step out of the room.

When we were called back in, the room had been darkened. In the center of the floor there were lit votive candles around a manger scene complete with Wise Men at

their destination. Around this, our group of twenty-four positioned ourselves and did yoga stretches, ending with the "child's pose" (kneeling on the floor, then lowering the body so that the belly rests on the thighs, the forehead is on the floor, and the arms are up-stretched beside the head). While we held this restful position, one of the instructors read a brief meditation. When we were finally invited to raise our heads, there was a glowing votive candle before each of us, between our extended hands: "The Light of the World, in each of us," she declared.

At the end of January, with my coursework successfully completed and my basic certificate in massage therapy stowed in my luggage, I returned home. I set up a studio in my house and began seeing massage clients on the days I wasn't working at the hospital. At first I offered just relaxing Swedish massages to friends and colleagues, but as I gained confidence, I took on clients with specific aches and pains, injuries, and emotional traumas. I even did several weeks of healing massage on the surgical site of a woman who'd recently had a radical mastectomy.

I continued my bodywork studies for another three years, learning craniosacral therapy, somatoemotional release, trigger-point work, shiatsu, and acupressure. In 1998, after I had returned to Berkeley for my master's degree in theology, I sat for and passed my National Certification Examination for Therapeutic Massage.

But if the whole point of all this work was to learn how to be with someone like Charlie, the AIDS patient who initiated my desire to learn massage, and to touch him in a way that would slake his thirst for compassionate touch as well as assuage my hunger to offer it, then what I had

sought was not to be found solely in anatomy and physiology classes, or Eastern modalities, or advanced Swedish massage. The reason I had needed to set out on this particular learning journey was to begin developing, in the words of the Care Through Touch training syllabus, the "spiritual practices that support . . . a compassionate ministry of touch." I needed to learn what I recorded one day in my massage training journal:

Two important lessons from today:
FEEL *what you are feeling*; and *Energy follows INTENT.*

I needed to be shown how to get out of the way of what could have happened of its own accord a year before, when my right hand held Charlie's right hand and my left hand rested gently on his shoulder.

TOUCH AS PRESENCE; PRESENCE AS TOUCH

The energy between Charlie and me had felt "stuck" because I had gotten in my own way. I'd thought there was something "more" that I needed to do, some mysterious action that could only be learned from someone who knew the secret. Until I took massage therapy training, I didn't understand that I didn't need to take massage therapy training—at least not for my original intentions.

All the requirements to learn physiology and anatomy, all the memorizing of massage sequences, all the learning of differences between *tapotement* and *petrissage*, and how muscle tissue feels different from ligament tissue under my fingers—all that would have helped me to touch Charlie in

more intelligent ways. All that training did help my hands to become more skilled. It allowed me to return to my chaplaincy work with a valuable title, *massage practitioner*, that became a kind of passport, allowing me to cross the barriers between myself and the people that I longed to touch in a healing way. But before I took the training, I hadn't understood that just being with Charlie, just resting my hand with intention anywhere on his body, would have been healing in itself.

Yet by studying Massage as the Art of Anointing, I learned that touch is far more expansive than solely what the hands do. I was "touching" Charlie in every moment and with every action of our coming together. I touched Charlie when I took a few seconds of silence to prepare myself before I entered his room. I touched Charlie when I put on the protective gown and mask as if they were beautiful, as if I didn't resent having to wear them. I touched him in the way I entered his room willingly, heartfully, noticing everything.

My eyes touched Charlie as they peered over my mask, taking in the details of his face, reading his mood, giving him time to read my eyes. I touched him in the manner in which I approached his bed slowly, intentionally, and in how I greeted him by touching his big toe respectfully and joyfully.

I straightened Charlie's sheets as if they were an extension of his body, and that was compassionate touch. I touched Charlie with the first words I said, and with how I listened to what he said and to the silences in between his words.

All of those actions are touch, all are part of the Art of

Anointing, and all, I now believe, are aspects of healing.

It is not necessary to be certified as a massage therapist to offer this kind of healing to a person in the margins. But to develop the art of compassionate presence, it is necessary to practice the skills of attention and intention. When you let your touch linger on a beggar's hand as you hand him a dollar, it takes those same essential skills that it takes to give a twenty-minute massage on the streets.

3

*I*n her profound little book *Perseverance*, Margaret Wheatley says that the secret to compassionate presence is this: "No questioning, no analysis, no distinctions— just bearing witness to what's present. The less we sort, judge, categorize or distinguish, the more we see and feel."

At its best, compassionate presence becomes a mutual endeavor, a conduit, a two-way exchange that flows easily. Sometimes the exchange is conscious, sometimes not.

When compassionate presence is flowing well, each side of the conduit offers something: a kind intention toward the other, or a willingness to risk being hurt by the other, or a step into dark spaces in the heart of the other, or a humility that acknowledges the reality of both equality and inequality.

When compassionate presence is flowing well, each side of the conduit also receives something: illumination of the hidden places inside oneself, or a long-held sorrow from the other's heart, or a kindness that might shatter one's well-built defenses, or a moment of healing.

When the compassionate conduit is open and flowing, each person can simply rest in the open-hearted presence of the other.

Margaret Wheatley agrees. "Without our usual filters

and boundaries," she writes, "we stop feeling repulsed or threatened or thrilled. We discover that we're much larger than our usual boundedness. In fact, we're big enough to take it all in."

But "filters and boundaries" are social habits, and they are difficult to shed. Human relating doesn't always work ideally. Blockages and barriers regularly get in the way of compassionate presence, and it's no surprise that a major barrier in relationships is fear. Fear can be like a ripe milkweed pod that has solidity and form, and you might think you can get a grip on it. But when pressure is put on the pod, it explodes into a thousand tiny parachutes, floating out in all directions, difficult to catch or find. The barrier of fear has a hundred aliases, including *shame, alienation, confusion, isolation, antipathy, vulnerability*.

And there are lots of other barriers to relationships as well. As I worked to be present in the margins, especially among the people of the streets, I experienced some unexpected, unique, and very memorable barriers.

What Gets in the Way

More often than not, massage practitioners who work through the Care Through Touch Institute work in pairs on the streets. It is safer, and more enjoyable, than doing the work solo.

I liked working with Dale. He had a colorful history that included some time living on the streets himself. He knew every alley and side street, every warehouse and railway siding and clump of bushes in the city. He could translate the graffiti spray-painted on walls. He knew the

location of every homeless encampment and how to access every hidey-hole under every overpass in San Francisco.

Service agencies would sometimes use Dale to find hidden homeless people, hoping to coax them into shelters during the cold, rainy months. Educated and with a wry sense of humor, he would arbitrarily take either side of a debate and sometimes subtly switch sides right in the middle of the conversation, just for the fun of putting his opponent off balance. Dale was a great teacher, making me rethink what I thought I knew about many things, but mostly about street life. He happily challenged me on all my assumptions about human nature.

Dale didn't do massage work; he transported those of us who did. He took us to some of the more remote places we wanted to go, and he stayed as our sentinel while we worked. Because he had been there himself and knew the body language as well as the patois of the streets, he often broke the ice for the practitioners, explaining what we did, introducing us to street people.

"Hey, man." (Pause, giving the street person time to size us up.)

"How ya doin'?" (Pause, offering space for a reply if there was one.)

"You livin' rough these days?" (Pause; the signs were clear that the person was living outdoors.)

"Ground gets pretty hard, don't it?" (Long pause, considering this together.)

"Back hurts like hell sometimes." (Pause, remembering; with body gestures to indicate aches and pains.)

"Well, this lady here, she's a massage therapist. Yeah, that's a fact. And she's here to give those aching shoulders

Cynthia Trenshaw

of yours a massage. If you want. Don't have to take off your shirt. You're fine just as you are." (Long pause to allow the person to consider what this might mean.)

"Sound like a good thing?"

At which point I'd move toward the homeless man, squat down to make eye contact, smile (but not too much), maybe rest my hand on his forearm while Dale was still talking (so the man could get a sense of my touch). There was a rhythm to it all, and mostly it was successful in making the connection we hoped for.

❧

Confronting My Personal History

Dale is a recovering alcoholic. We talk sometimes about that disease, so he knows that I have uncomfortable childhood memories around alcoholism. I try to be careful in our conversations, so that my history and opinions don't come off sounding like judgments of him.

We are a good team, Dale and I. Except for one thing: he seems to love setting me up to work on alcoholics, preferably when they are under the influence. He can find them unerringly. And if he has already made the offer of a massage to the person, I can't un-offer it. I am obliged to follow through, even though I might be repulsed by the drunken body I am massaging.

It is almost as if Dale were daring me to dislike this person, daring me to dislike Dale himself, for his disease. Where is my vaunted "compassionate

touch" then? What is the value of my "spiritual practice" when all I want is to get away from this person as quickly as possible? But here I stand, committed to a course of action that challenges every good thing I believe about myself. Because he's done it to me again.

As I approach the man Dale has set up for me (or set me up for!), tag ends of old, ugly memories swirl in my chest like dry brown oak leaves, sucked loose by the smell of stale alcohol. I can feel my older brother leaning heavily, like a wounded soldier, on my pre-teen shoulders, slurring his plea to help him find his bed. I can see my gentle father, fabricating once again his story about needing to "check on the furnace," behind which his current bottle is stashed. I see our family tiptoeing around the lies. Less clearly I remember my step-grandfather, his huge hands callused by a lifetime of farming; I see his black razor strop made shiny from daily use, threatening in its wordless presence on a hook beside the kitchen sink. For a moment I mourn the minds of my male role models, thoroughly marinated before I ever got to know them well.

The man Dale has chosen is sitting on the grass. I kneel behind him on a gardener's foam kneepad. I am repelled by the sticky, arrogant energy of this alcoholic homeless man with his back turned to me expectantly. I repeat that he should keep his sweatshirt on; I'll work through the fabric. He is chuckling at some private joke, and his breath reeks. Yet I place my hands on his shoulders. I search for an untainted patch of air to inhale deeply as I begin my work. I strain to hear a bird call—almost always in the city there is a bird somewhere, even if it's just a pigeon or a gull—any sound to connect me with what is natural and whole.

And then it begins: my palms sink just a little into his shoulders as the man's musculature starts to relax. How long has it been since he's been touched gently? Slowly but firmly I slide my hands out from his shoulders and down his arms and then gently drag my fingers back up to his shoulders. When I repeat that motion, he tries to lean back and snuggle his scapulae against my breasts. I hold his shoulders securely and say firmly, "Don't," and he obeys. When I press my thumbs in small circles on both sides of the length of his spine, he leans forward and cradles his head on his arms folded over his knees. My left hand steadies his body as the heel of my right hand traces the curve of his back over his ribs; I imagine pushing away and discarding his pain and anger and failure and sickness. I repeat the sequence on his left side. In this moment the man whom Dale has bestowed on me is no longer repulsive to me; he is vulnerable in his human need for kindness and healing. In that need he and I, and Dale as well, are one.

❧

I'd like to say that I learned not to be bothered by alcoholic behaviors, but that would not be true. What I did learn was to keep on searching for compassion in the midst of my discomfort. I learned not to let my own squirming set up a barrier to potential healing. And I had yet another chat with Dale about how I did not appreciate what he'd done to me—again.

But I didn't always need Dale to get me into uncomfortable predicaments. It wasn't always he who set up situations that contained blockages and barriers.

Often enough I managed that all by myself.

❧

"Imprudence"—
A Refined Word for Bumbling

Sometimes, in order to give seated massages on the streets, a practitioner has to "prime the pump" to find folks willing to receive a massage. Spot just one person who looks likely to agree to a massage and, if you've guessed right, you can be sure that a dozen other street folks will be watching both the giver and the receiver and making up their minds about whether they'd be willing to get touched like that. Often I'd look for someone I recognized, someone I'd worked with before, to smooth the way for an afternoon's work. A friend once said this seemed like "benevolent seduction," yet there was nothing sexual or commercial about it. This was just a way to help potential receivers see how the work was done.

One afternoon early in my career of street work, I was by myself at a place on Market Street where there was no one I recognized. But I noticed a small woman in a wheelchair.

Her long gray hair is woven into a thick braid down the middle of her back. Half a dozen bulky plastic bags, a signature of homelessness, fill her lap and hang from the handles of her wheelchair. She is facing away from me, talking animatedly to a circle of several friends. I am moved, seeing how they care for her. She seems like a great person to start with today; there is even a built-in audience of potential massage-receivers.

So I walk over to the circle, stepping in beside her to allow her to see me. I put my hand gently on her shoulder, introduce myself, and offer her a massage. But there is something strange about her expression. And, now that I have looked more fully around the circle, there is something strange about the expressions of her attentive friends as well. All conversation has ceased. I feel as if I've stepped into a collectively held breath.

In fact, I believe that what I have done, in my naivety, is to walk right into a large, probably lucrative drug deal. I don't know how I know it, but that's what's registering in my gut.

Who is this broad? the people surrounding me seem to be wondering. *If she were a cop, we'd know; therefore she's not a cop. So who could possibly be this stupid? Slowly I turn back to the old woman in the wheelchair, take my hand off her entrepreneurial shoulder, smile at her, and say, "Maybe another day would be better." Then I leave the circle and the vicinity as fast as I can, chagrinned and a little bit scared.*

❧

I learned from my embarrassment with the woman in the wheelchair. My unsophisticated self began to notice other street enterprises. I learned to recognize prostitutes pretty easily, because the success of being a hooker depends on overt marketing, and practitioners are not interested in my kind of massage while they're at work. I noticed shoplifting, but kept my own counsel about it. Then I got good at spotting plainclothes police by how they used their eyes like radar; I became skilled at not getting between the cops and anyone who held their interest.

❧

Protective Padding

Sometimes the barriers to massage, particularly on the streets, are composed not of memories or emotions or cultural naivety; some barriers are physical. The tortuous routes that lead to deeply hidden encampments, or the ubiquitous bags of trash that hinder passage in an alleyway, or the difficult angle of approach to an aching shoulder when its owner is sitting on a crowded sidewalk—all can be physical barriers.

And then there is the barrier of excessive clothing. A person who doesn't have a place to call home might have to carry all their worldly possessions on their back—literally. Such was the case with Teddy, who hung out in Boeddeker Park.

Boeddeker Park is a great idea that mostly doesn't work. It was named for a beloved Franciscan priest, Father Alfred Boeddeker, who founded St. Anthony's Services for homeless people. The park was designed to keep children and families safe for a few hours from the vagaries of the streets. Sadly, even with the Tenderloin police station right across the street, the park's fences and gates serve more to keep crime in and kids and innocent people out.

That never seems to deter Teddy. Every day, no matter what the weather is, no matter what drugs are being sold or fights are happening at the lower end of the park, Teddy will be sitting at a concrete table at the park's upper end.

Regardless of the day's temperature, Teddy will be wearing all of the clothes that he owns. Teddy isn't his real name, but it's what he is called on the street because, wearing all those layers, he looks like a stuffed teddy bear. Sometimes his daily duds include four pairs of trousers, half a dozen shirts, and five or six jackets. This mode of dressing saves him from having to push a cart around, and makes it less likely that he'll get ripped off—it just isn't worth a thief's time to paw through all that clothing. And heaven only knows what it smells like down near the inner layers.

You might wonder how a massage therapist could make any difference through all that clothing. You might wonder why she'd risk her olfactory sensitivities to the aromas brewing closer to the skin. The simple truth is that Teddy dearly loves massages. Sometimes I can convince him to take off a few of his jackets so he can better appreciate his massage, but that's about the most he's ever agreed to. The fact is that it is I who think I know how things should be done, when it is actually Teddy who knows what needs to happen. All those layers keep Teddy's odors contained, but they do not confine his goodness and his longing. They do not prevent the essence of Teddy from reaching up to me, to meet my hands and my intention.

The moment I touch him, Teddy leans forward and puts his head on his arms on the table, and I focus all my intention on the musculature of Teddy's back and shoulders, visualizing the anatomy hidden deep inside all those layers of cloth and stuffing.

There is no way I can reach deep enough to touch that anatomy, so with my hands moving on top of his duct-tape-repaired quilted jacket, I close my eyes and "invite" Teddy's

anatomy up to meet my palms. It is almost as if the clothing slowly yields from below and from above, and then disappears entirely.

With the gentlest of movements, so as not to break the fragile energetic connection between us, I massage what my hands and fingers and imagination perceive: spine, neck, shoulders, scapulae, rotator cuffs, upper arms, forearms, even the wrists and the joints of the fingers inside his gloves— it's all there, all hidden, all hungrily soaking up attention and compassion.

This unusual arrangement works for both Teddy and me; after fifteen minutes of being together in this odd sort of touching, Teddy sighs deeply, then trundles off happily to the soup kitchen. And I feel as satisfied with my work as if I just gave a spectacular full-body massage.

❧

Revulsion

There are times when a street person is so filthy, so ill, so drunk, so angry, so feral and seemingly non-human that there is no way any sane person would approach him, no way any sane person would touch him. Those were the times when I was glad to have a partner trained in street work. She could help me by:

1. Confirming that on this day this person really is nasty and should be passed by, or

2. Challenging the "nasty" assumption and appealing to guilt, spiritual practices, or numerous other factors to get me to reconsider, or

3. Doing the massage herself if we "flipped" for it
 and she lost.

The day I gave a massage to Jay, I hadn't been sure
that I could do it. At first, when we approached Jay,
my partner and I had done our silent assessment
(urine-soaked pants, vomit on shirt, probably lice in
tangled hair). We did our invisible "coin toss" with
a glance at each other, and I "lost" the toss by
looking down first, thus conceding. My partner
moved off to the side, smiling as if to say, He's all
yours.

*Jay might be thirty, might be fifty. He is wrapped in a
shredded gray blanket, lying on a bench in a little pocket park
near San Francisco's Embarcadero. Tall, luxurious hotels and
the financial district of the city loom around him; traffic sighs
without ceasing on the double-decked Bay Bridge, which
soars a few blocks to the southeast, and buses and trucks rumble
on the multiple-lane streets surrounding the small patch of
green. But here in the sun, beneath a few trees, it is peaceful.*

*Jay watches me warily as I approach. He sees a gray-
haired woman in jeans, a colorful jacket, dangling earrings,
and running shoes. She is a stranger who looks at him
directly, which is odd. She tells him she's a massage therapist.
Then she kneels down and asks the strangest question: Would
he like to have a neck and shoulder massage? He is uncertain,
suspicious. Why would this person want to touch him? Does
she know he has lice, and that last night he vomited on his
shirt and he had no clean change of clothes?*

I continue to make eye contact with him, and smile

gently. Slowly Jay sits up on the bench, thinks a little longer, then says, "Yeah."

Jay can't sleep at night anymore. One night last year, as he dozed in a doorway near Washington Square, he was mugged by two young men. He was beaten with sticks and slashed with a broken bottle. Now he is scared and hyper-alert to the dangers that night brings for homeless people. When the sun rises and most of us wake for the day, Jay is exhausted and aching, longing for safe sleep.

I spread disinfectant on my hands, so he knows I do not carry contagions from my last massage. Then I move to stand behind him, and rest my palms on his shoulders. For just a second I pause, centering myself and wishing this man peace through my touch.

Now that I have touched Jay, I feel my attention sink into his unsoiled essence. The vomit smell, the scabies, the still-damp urine stains on his trousers, even the lice scurrying deeper into his blond dreadlocks as I massage his head, all become superficial details tacked onto the exquisite, fragile human condition that we share.

The moment my hands begin to knead his muscles, he sighs and his body starts to relax. For a while he will float in a world of nurturing touch, healing possibilities, and safety. And so will I, for though I do not understand how it happens (and it's more or less a secret well-kept by massage therapists), the locus where givers and receivers of massage meet is mutual. One cannot touch without being touched. One cannot create a space of safety without feeling safe within it. One cannot heal without being touched by healing. Because I am focused on my work and truly "in" it, whatever Jay experiences I experience as well.

Jay is unaware of the dozens of people passing by on their lunchtime way from shops and offices to cafés and street vendors. My day's partner, another massage practitioner from the Care Through Touch Institute, is watching protectively from a few yards away. Later she will describe to me the passersby and how they respond as they glance at a filthy homeless man being massaged: some seem to be disgusted and angry that anyone would encourage someone like Jay. Some seem bemused, wondering how this connection happened. Some stop and stare and appreciate, smiling at the woman who has the courage to touch Jay and the skill to ease the tension in his muscles.

It is not my intention to do performance art. I am only vaguely aware of any of these people. Instead, I am deep in conversation with Jay's body, its musculature and its energy, finding the places that cry out for compassionate human touch. I do not care that the angriest of the passersby resent what I'm doing: left alone lying on his bench, Jay would have remained invisible to them. But because someone from their "class" of people is touching him, they have been forced to notice him. Their attention has been arrested by an anomaly: their seeing has traced the path from my visible middle-class face and down my arms, to my hands, to the formerly hidden one upon whom my hands rest. The passersby have noticed destitution. I believe that is a good thing even though they resent it.

When the massage is finished, I bow slightly toward Jay's back, acknowledging the sacred time we've shared. Then I go around to sit in front of him, waiting for him to "come back" to himself on this patch of parkland. He opens his eyes. Like the passersby, he's uncertain how to respond to what he's just

experienced. He mutters, "Thank you. I'll be able to sleep now. Thank you. God bless you."

"You're very welcome, Jay." And I mean that, because for the past half hour I've been in the same unlikely place of bliss that he has.

❧

But blissful does not mean unwise. After I'd walked away out of Jay's sight, I stripped off my jacket, folding the outside of it tightly into the middle. I walked the six blocks to where my car was parked, so I could throw my wadded-up jacket into the trunk, hoping that any hitchhiking critters would remain captured there until I could annihilate them in the hot water of my washing machine.

My hair, pulled up into a knot at the back of my head, had not touched Jay's matted hair, so the lice were not a genuine concern. I knew that I had not had enough skin-to-skin contact to worry about scabies boring into my arms, and I had a window of time before that could happen anyway. Nevertheless, my imagination was already starting to make my arms itch. I headed for the nearest hotel lobby restroom to scrub my hands and arms. Then my partner and I walked back out into the afternoon. There was no question of who would "win" the next imaginary coin toss. The barrier of revulsion lessens with time and experience, but it never goes away entirely—it is only more easily tolerated.

The barriers to compassionate connection are
elusive and seem endless; as soon as one sort is
recognized and weeded out, another crops up that
looks nothing like the one before. My painful
memories of alcoholism didn't at all help me to
recognize a drug deal. Recognizing a drug deal
didn't at all resemble the four-inch thickness of
Teddy's clothing. Teddy's clothing was nothing
compared to the protective emotional "armoring"
of several prostitutes whom I massaged in a
transitional safe house. They were willing to remove
their clothing for a full-body massage, but it was
unlikely that most would ever be able, like Teddy, to
let compassion penetrate the barricades they'd built
around their psyches. And approaching their
modestly draped, clean bodies on a massage table
in a safe house was not at all like approaching Jay's
filthy body on a park bench. I hadn't known it at
the time, but this learning to recognize the barriers
and to overcome whatever stands in the way of the
flow of compassionate touch was the primary
lesson I had sought to learn in massage therapy
training.

That, and this: The intention behind the touch
is what makes compassionate touch possible. The
intention behind one's presence is what makes
compassionate presence possible.

4

I N T E N T I O N

To survive life on the streets, homeless people must develop whole new sets of skills different from the ones that served them previously.

Perhaps she once worked with columns of numbers on her computer all day, but on the streets she must instead have a finely tuned sense of hearing, an instant alertness to the presence and the meaning of any particular sound in the general din.

Maybe he once actively climbed ladders, hauled shingles, and pounded nails each day, but on the streets he must instead develop a patience for inertia and standing in end-less lines for every daily necessity from a toilet to a sandwich.

If she once worked in a neonatal unit tending newborns with unseasoned, anonymous faces, on the streets she must instead be able to read each line and tic of every face to discern the underlying meaning and intention of their approach.

Whatever else they may know or have learned on the street, almost any homeless person can sense *intention* from a dozen paces away. Morse Putnam Strawbridge, a character in Kevin Brockmeier's novel *The Illumination*, is a homeless man who sells books on a blanket on the streets. Of him the author writes:

The Readers and the Good Samaritans—that was who he wanted. He could identify the Good Samaritans from half a block away, zeroing in on him in a fury of benevolence, their fingers sharp and rigid, but the Readers were harder to spot.

If you're open to being with Morse, just as he is in this moment, you—just as you are in this moment—may find a place to sit beside him. If you're coming to change him, to fix him, he will retract his real self deep inside, away from your "fury of benevolence."

The intention to "fix" includes an assumption of brokenness; seeing a person as "broken" and "needy" means you already have negative judgments about her: she is defective in some way. And seeing a person as defective is a judgment that helps create the margins in the first place.

Like Morse Putnam Strawbridge, no one wants to be told that they are deficient by another's attitude of superiority or do-goodism. In *Walden*, Henry David Thoreau says: "If I knew for a certainty that a man was coming to my house with the conscious design of doing me good, I should run for my life."

BEING WITH

I was on the streets regularly between the years of 1996 and 2001. In order to work there, I, like a person who lives there, had to learn a new set of skills. To bring compassionate touch to homeless people required that I turn my training upside down, and have no expectations, no intentions at all.

In my regular massage therapy practice, my clients and

I expected changes in their bodies as a result of our work together. A spasming calf muscle would be convinced to relax, and its pain eased; a repetitive strain injury in a wrist would respond to manipulation of the many wrist bones, giving the compressed nerves space to heal; a week's worth of tension would melt away under slow, deep *petrissage*. But on the streets my expectations had to change. My intentions had to change. It was the perfect Zen meditation: beginner's mind, blank slate. I might not even get to touch the person I approached, let alone "fix" anything about them. Just to make eye contact was an accomplishment; to be with, and to talk, was a victory. To touch was for later, if ever.

Even my understanding of presence had to be altered on the streets. The right to be with could not be assumed; it had to be earned and granted. When I worked as a chaplain, there were assumptions vested in the title engraved on my name badge, and I had come to believe that my presence could make a change for the better in the patients I saw. In fact, that was often true. But patients and their families, and even some staff, assumed that I had God's private cellphone number and that when my caller ID showed up on the screen, God would be more likely to answer the current prayer. And they assumed that, because I was part of the hospital staff, I had a right to enter any room in the institution regardless of whether the patient wanted me there or not. Though I was acutely sensitive to a patient's receptivity (or lack of it), there was still a sense of entitlement that came with my job. That attitude was cured on the streets.

On the streets compassionate presence and nonjudg-

Cynthia Trenshaw

ment have to precede a person like a perfume, like a pheromone, announcing openness and curiosity and welcome. Nothing about "changing" or "fixing." "Fixing" is not the point at all. "Being with" is the point. "Seeing deeply" is the point. "Learning from" is the point. Mostly there is nothing that can be fixed anyway. And even compassionate presence can have no expectations about its own quality or purpose. It simply is, a part of the mystery of compassion, of "feeling with."

❧

PLEASE HELP—

Muther with 3 smal kids

There is a place in San Francisco, beneath the Central Freeway, where steel and concrete pillars form a surreal forest. Those urban trunks support six lanes of freeway traffic that rumbles incessantly overhead, creating a sonic tunnel below. Another six lanes of city streets stream through that lower acoustic corridor, three on either side of the supporting pillars. The upper freeway traffic is ceaseless; the street traffic below is stop-and-go, interrupted at every block by cross streets and stoplights. The cars and trucks move on, but what they spew has no place to go, and so it stays. Carbon monoxide and diesel smoke and litter fill the artery, trapped among the echoes of car horns, engine revs, and brake squeals.

This place is all shadowy gray. Concrete gray. Broken-glass gray. Last-week's-newspaper gray. A gray safety island lies between the three-lane halves of the street under the freeway. Concrete pillars rise on either end of the island, like

48

stiff palm trees for an urban castaway. As the base of one of the pillars there is a broken metal folding chair, a filthy pillowcase lumpy with crammed clothing, and a small plastic bucket and an overturned milk crate, both red—the only non-gray in the scene.

And there is a woman. Though she is young, she seems gray, too. Her long hair might be blond except for the soot. Her clothes might be colorful except for the dirt and stench, but her skin is probably grayish even beneath the smudges. She has propped a cardboard sign on the broken chair; it wavers in the slipstreams of rushing cars. The handwritten block letters plead: *PLEASE HELP, Muther with 3 smal kids!*

She sits on the red milk crate, holding the small red bucket, trying to panhandle both sides of the safety island from her plastic perch even though she is barely able to remain upright. She is a heroin user who recently mainlined her drug. Dodging traffic, I approach her from behind, then move around in front so as not to startle her. I brush broken glass off the concrete, move her needle to the side, and kneel to look into her heavy-lidded eyes. I tell her my name and that I am a massage therapist. "Would you like for me to massage your neck and shoulders, to get some of the kinks out of them?" I ask.

For a while she stares at me, considering. "How much?" she asks. It is the most frequent question I get in a day out here.

"It doesn't cost anything. I'm just here to massage your back." Yet I know it will cost us both dearly. She will have to rummage in her pockets for courage, allowing me to touch her with a tenderness she can't afford to believe in anymore. I will have to pay with eyes that see myself in her gray face.

And I'll have to try to dig deep, to unfold the currency of enough compassion for us both.

"Why?" she asks. The second-most frequent question.

"Because I want to be here with you." Maybe the "why" is that some part of the Golden Rule is genetically encoded into both of us. But my own answer is more like the mountain-climber's response: because you are here, and because I can.

A motorist stopping for a red light dangles a dollar bill through a one-inch opening in his window; she wobbles up, retrieves it, and sits back down. "Whadda I hafta do?"

"Nothing except sit here. And let me know if anything I do doesn't feel good."

She studies my eyes as best she can, then moves her left shoulder a few inches toward me, indicating that I should start there. I move around to stand behind her, rest my hands on her shoulders for a moment so she gets a sense of herself and me connected to each other by touch. Such a confusion of messages meets my hands: tension, hunger for release, resistance, and the electric buzz of her drug rewiring her nervous system. I breathe in, then press my thumbs into those matched points in the trapezius muscle that seem to be the gatekeepers to all of a body's tensions.

As I knead her shoulders and upper arms, she begins to relax. Or maybe the heroin is taking her deeper. It doesn't matter. Her eyes are closed when another dollar is offered; I prop her up against my hip and hold out her red bucket— wouldn't want to let one get away. Then, when I cup her forehead in my left hand and work the muscles of her neck with my right, a driver stops and yells, "What's wrong?"

"Nothing," I say. "I'm giving her a massage."

"You're nuts!" he yells, and guns through the green light.

Twenty minutes later, my hands gently lift from her shoulders. The gray woman can barely rouse herself. Helping her to her feet, I gather her nest egg of alms from the red bucket and stuff it into her pants pocket. She sways, and I catch her. I hand her the cardboard sign and her bucket, and cram the pillowcase into the milk crate. But I can't manage the broken chair along with the milk crate and the woman, so the chair gets left behind on the island.

The walk light flashes permission, and I guide the woman to the shore on the other side of the river of traffic. Halfway down the next block there is an empty lot, fenced in with chain-link, with a patch of dry weeds between the fence and the sidewalk. There I put her red crate and her belongings. There I put her, and tell her goodbye. There is nothing more I can do to comfort her. It will be several more hours before the heroin leaves her veins, and the lack will rouse her.

"Thanks," she says. She wants so much to say more, but the words get lost somewhere. So she says it again: "Thanks." My heart warms, and I wish fervently that I could change her life for her. But I remember that I'm not the one in charge of lives. I am here simply to be present to, and to appreciate, the imperfect beauty of what is before me.

I walk away, toward the gray tunnel of fumes and noise and concrete. The evening's fog is just beginning to spill over the edges of the freeway, chilly and damp. The front door of my home will look very welcoming tonight.

❧

Massage had not been the real point of my going to that concrete island. "Massage" was simply my excuse. Offering massage provided a rationale for my staying with the gray

woman and touching her; it helped her to be less afraid of me; it helped me to be less afraid of being there. But the point of my being with this woman was to let her know she was seen, to touch her as a way of confirming her realness and worth, and perhaps my own as well.

I had thought that years of training and thousands of dollars of tuition were a necessary foundation for me to do what I was doing, but that turned out not to be true. Of course, I found that out only after I'd already spent the years and the dollars! All in search of training for some "useful" skill, some way of helping, socially acceptable and intellectually satisfying, that was validated by framed certificates displayed on my walls.

Yet it turned out that just being me was enough.

And the gray woman: just as she was, she was enough.

Whatever it was that happened in our exchange that day was enough.

I was beginning to understand that that is the ideal perception, the ideal intention: simply to be enough.

5

H AVING E NOUGH

By definition, people who are homeless or ill or destitute or dying do not have enough. They haven't enough reliable shelter or enough health or enough money or enough remaining life. In our culture most of them have been edged out of our awareness toward the more marginal spaces: retirement complexes, low-income apartments, nursing homes, the streets. Even if they can still cling to the lifestyle they've known, they are afraid that they are slipping toward the edge of isolation and disdain.

"Having enough" of health or shelter or money or possessions is temporal and fragile. One illness, an accident, or a financial mistake can shatter what we consider the condition of "enough." Down deep we know this, and we can be haunted by the specter of scarcity even in the midst of our current abundance.

Some days, after working with homeless people or dying people, and recognizing how close I could be, daily, to losing everything, I just wallow in the fear. Sometimes I can shake it off or distract myself with other thoughts, or a book or a movie or a glass of wine. And sometimes, in sweet moments of insight, I become overwhelmed with gratitude for the possessions and the choices I do have, right now, right here, in this instant. I revel in my

abundance, feel gratitude for everything from my bank account to my doorknobs.

～

Meditation on Abundance

Focus on it: a doorknob. I am so grateful for a doorknob. Specifically, the doorknob in my own door, that attaches to a latch that catches into a solid doorframe in the wall of my home. That doorknob lets me close my door on whichever side of it I choose. I can close unwanted people out for privacy, or welcome friends in for companionship, or close my posses-sions in for security.

And I'm grateful for the walls. Before I worked in nursing homes and hospitals, I didn't fully appreciate walls made of wood and plaster, not cloth. Before I became familiar with the people of the streets I didn't understand how it might be to have no walls, no doorframe, no door, no latch, no doorknob.

Or no toilet paper.

In my bathroom I have soft, white, perforated squares of toilet paper, rolled up, waiting for whenever I need them. I don't have to ask a shelter official for my daily allotment— it's already there. For me. Beside my toilet. My beautiful, flushable toilet. With a seat. Fifteen inches above the floor so I needn't squat uncomfortably to use it. There are no lines of people waiting to use my toilet ahead of me when my body's needs are urgent. There are no one else's feces, urine, blood, cigarette butts, or used needles embellishing it. My toilet is clean and ready. Behind a door. Imagine having more than one door! What joy!

Next to my toilet there is a shower. I can go into my shower whenever I want; I don't have to wait for a nursing home aide to haul me to my scheduled bathing time. In my shower I have scented soap and shampoo and a clean washcloth. My shower's plumbing comes with two handles, one marked cold *and one marked* hot, *and each reliably brings to me the water it promises, clean and abundant. In the tiled floor of the shower is a drain that carries away my body's dirt, the soap scum, and the shampoo bubbles laced with stray hairs. I don't need to dispose of these things—the drain does it for me. I watch it work and feel great gratitude.*

I am grateful for my quilted mattress, a full forty inches wide, covered by fresh sheets whenever I wish, and blankets that are still dry and warm when I wake in the morning. I have a soft pillow filled with feathers, not ancient foam crunchy from sweat and grime. I have a lamp beside my bed and a place to plug it in, and I can leave it on as long as I like. I have chairs to sit in, and bookshelves filled with my books and memorabilia that please me. I can pile my things on my floor if I want, and no one tells me I can't, and I don't have to carry them all around with me so they're not stolen or thrown away.

And get this: I've even got a refrigerator that keeps my food from spoiling and a stove to cook my own meal and a table to hold everything while I eat with metal, not plastic, utensils! I can choose what I eat, and when, and with whom I eat or whether I can have fresh vegetables! Thank you. Thank you. Thank you.

❧

How did I come to have such luxury?

How long will I have it?

And if one day I don't have my own toilet paper, if I don't have fresh food or an internet connection, will there be any point in going on? If I were mentally ill, or physically ill, or handicapped, or afraid all the time, or shunned by those who seem to live a safe distance from the margins, would I despair? And when, not *if*, I become old—instead of suffering day after day, won't I just want to end it all?

Well, some do that. Suicide on the streets happens more than twice as often as the national average. Elders in our society—not just those who are homeless—particularly white males over the age of eighty-five, complete suicide at nearly six times the national average. And some marginalized people check out more slowly than suicide, choosing instead to ingest or inject whatever will bring blessed numbness temporarily, but still allow another day to dawn —perhaps a better day, or perhaps not.

But what if *enough* were redefined? In *The Soul of Money*, Lynn Twist offers this perspective:

> We each have the choice in any setting to step back and let go of the mind-set of scarcity. Once we let go of scarcity, we discover the surprising truth of sufficiency. By sufficiency, I don't mean a quantity of anything. Sufficiency isn't two steps up from poverty or one step short of abundance. It isn't a measure of barely enough or more than enough. Sufficiency isn't an amount at all. It is an experience, a context we generate, a declaration, a knowing that there is enough, and that we are enough.

Or what if *enough* were objectively comparative, not subjective? Compared to the people of other, undeveloped, countries, even the homeless people of the American margins have plenty.

But if one had no doorknob or toilet or computer or roof, could there be good reasons to fall asleep one night and actually hope to wake up the next morning?

There could and there are, and they surprise me often.

Despite what I expect, people of the margins, who have already lost so much of their ability to choose, nevertheless often choose to see their lives through a lens of plenty.

ENCAMPMENTS: THE MARGINS OF THE MARGINS

An *encampment* is a hidden-away, otherwise-unused space that is temporarily homesteaded by homeless people. It may be under a viaduct, at an alleyway dead-end, or in a vacant lot in the warehouse district.

୶

"Being Settled"

Beneath the Bay Bridge ramp between Third and Fourth Streets, there is a collection of construction equipment and materials. It is a cold, wet afternoon. On a four-foot-wide space between some plywood fencing and a huge yellow bulldozer, two wooden pallets are covered with stacked corrugated cardboard and old blankets. A man and a woman are napping there, hidden away from the world by the giant yellow machine. Nancy, my outreach partner today, calls our approach, and the couple rouses. I recognize Amanda as she

sits up. I remember first meeting her at United Nations Plaza four months earlier, just after she'd had a baby that she gave up for adoption. As the other person comes out from under the blankets I recognize him too, from a day shelter: Jerry. Both of them are in their mid-twenties. They welcome us, genuinely glad to see us again.

The detritus surrounding their sleeping space contains soft drink cups, cigarette butts, fast food wrappers, and blood-soaked paper towels and tampons. Good, I think. She's not yet pregnant again. Amanda and Jerry are celebrating the three-month anniversary of their relationship, and offer us a sip from their bottle of wine. We say we can't, thanks; we're working.

Amanda gets frequent headaches and Jerry often has shoulder pain. They have tried to duplicate the ways we massaged them, wanting to do for each other what we did for them, and they demonstrate for us what they remember. Then, as the rain drips from the freeway overhead, we massage each of them while they both observe carefully. All four of us chat in the little home they've made for themselves. They've used the steps and ledges and indentations of the bulldozer as shelves for organizing their food and belongings, pleased that they've been here for four days without anyone forcing them to move on.

This is "being settled" in the world of homeless people.

For Amanda and Jerry, for today, it is enough.

❧

There was a small encampment Nancy and I knew of in another part of town, but when we arrived that afternoon, we found nobody home. What we did find were several

notices duct-taped to the overpass pillars, written in English and Spanish:

NOTICE OF REMOVAL OF PROPERTY
ILLEGALLY PLACED ON STATE RIGHT OF WAY

Property remaining on this location on 04/20/00 is subject to disposal.

REMOVE YOUR PROPERTY IMMEDIATELY.

Telephone (510) 286-6444 regarding stored property.
Date Notice was Posted: 04/17/00
Location of Posted Notice: Rincon Hill 080

The encampment had been evicted. No one is surprised when this happens; the surprise comes when folks are allowed to take root for more than a few days.

I had developed an attitude about the cops who roust people from the places where they are just beginning to feel at home or tell them to "move on" when they are too exhausted to do so. Then, one hot spring day, on a southern edge of Golden Gate Park, I watched two officers waking a man who was sleeping on the sidewalk with his back against the brick wall of an apartment building. I asked one of them why they couldn't just leave the guy alone while he slept.

"Ma'am," he said, "let me show you something." While his partner talked with the homeless man, who was now on his feet and walking toward the park, the cop had me kneel down where the man had been lying. The sidewalk and the wall were blistering hot. "If we leave him here for long, he'll dehydrate, maybe die," the cop said.

He was right, of course. I thanked him for his kindness. Now the homeless man could live for another day, transplanted to the shade beneath a rhododendron bush in the park. That would be his sleeping shelter; he would sober up by nightfall and probably find food by dumpster-diving in the Haight-Ashbury neighborhood. By tomorrow morning he might look back and declare today to have been "okay." He did, after all, have enough.

୰

China Basin Encampment

One late autumn afternoon, with no advance discussion, I am asked by Doug, case manager for the Mission Rock Shelter, to go with him to do outreach at a nearby homeless encampment. On any given day Doug is either a curmudgeon or a teddy bear—sometimes both at once. He is well respected among the homeless population because he has a deeply caring, no-nonsense heart formed by his own life's experiences of addictions and homelessness. At Mission Rock, Doug has mostly ignored me and sometimes watched my massage work without comment. Apparently, I have passed his personal litmus test, for he is now going to risk taking me with him to a large encampment.

An encampment is not a place to be afraid, necessarily, but it is a place to exercise due caution and keen senses. Doug instructs me never to go to this place by myself. "If you get your throat slit, at least I want to know where to tell the coroner to look for you," he says, and I am not sure what percentage of that is just his dark humor.

This encampment looks and smells like a garbage heap.

In fact it is a garbage heap, but worse: I've been told that this particular many-acre site has several acres of toxic waste as its base, covered over by thousands of cubic yards of garbage, trash, dirt, and broken concrete. Fragile cardboard and tarp dwellings for more than a hundred people perch on its surface. Whenever the authorities leave them alone for more than a day or two, homeless people can create ingenious living spaces, a nascent governing and supply infrastructure, and even a community sorted into social subdivisions. This encampment has been left alone for several weeks, and is well entrenched and diverse.

Doug and I have walked down Third Avenue, crossed a bridge over a polluted inlet from the Bay, and turned left onto a path beside the water. Thirty yards farther, where the encampment begins, the first person we encounter is Marie—mentally ill, grossly overweight, and shy. She is eating dry cornflakes out of a plastic Pepsi cup, outside her "hootch," a tent made of blankets. Doug introduces me. Marie has experienced massage once before, in a shelter, and she is eager to receive one again. While I massage her shoulders and neck and arms, Doug moves among the lean-tos and sleeping bags, handing out sandwiches and fruit from Mission Rock Shelter and trying to convince folks to come to the shelter before the city follows through on its threat to evict them from the encampment, and before the winter rains turn the dump into a toxic mud swamp.

When Marie's massage is finished, I hug her. She is teary-eyed, and I ask if she is okay. She is, and she is not, of course; it was a stupid question. The tears aren't because she isn't okay—the tears are because she's just experienced a few rare moments of being okay, and the contrast aches.

In this encampment, people with severe mental and physical and addictive illnesses attach themselves to the perimeter of the community, at the edge farthest from Third Avenue. This is, I suppose, the ultimate margin: the isolated verge of a homeless encampment on the fringes of society. Even here, however, folks look out for one another in a cursory way—if someone scores big in a grocery dumpster, the food might be shared. If someone is badly injured, word goes to the homeless woman who was once a nurse, and she is asked to look at the injury. If a trip to the emergency room is required, someone will probably come up with a bus token, and maybe even accompany the ill or injured person as far as the emergency room doors. At this end of the encampment, Doug and I distribute sandwiches and the shelter invitation/eviction warning to any who emerge from under their cardboard and blankets. But not many do, and we respect people's privacy.

We pick our way toward the Latino section, the encampment's "high-rent district." Here several wood-and-plastic-walled hootches are clustered together around a small courtyard protected by a large blue tarp. Four men in the courtyard are playing cards on a folding table that's missing one leg. In one of the huts a black-and-white television blares—someone has spliced into the wires at the base of a street lamp a few hundred feet away and thus brought electricity to the camp. Doug uses his limited Spanish (I have none) and gestures to explain why I am there. We are both surprised when one of the card players accepts a massage. Even more unexpectedly, his buddies, instead of making fun of him, pause in their game and watch respectfully, even reverently, the whole time I work. It is easy to forget that these people are the human detritus of San Francisco, living

on top of the industrial, commercial detritus of a culture that does not recognize "enough." Doug leaves the last of the apples and sandwiches, along with a final invitation to "come inside," and we return to Mission Rock Shelter.

❧

People who live in shelters don't get to choose whom they live with; they don't get to make the rules they must abide by. That's one reason why some prefer to live in communal encampments or, when they can, live alone. That was Jim's choice: being alone, or with a few people of his own choosing, keeping his own schedule and making his own rules. He created for himself, and for a handful of others, a world that was bountiful and beautiful, and more than just "enough." I was privileged to become one of Jim's friends, and when finally I moved away from the Bay Area, it was parting from my beloved Jim that was the most wrenching leave-taking of all.

❧

Jim:
Making Home and Hospitality Every Day

After the San Francisco stores have closed for the day and the downtown office workers have scuttled away to their homes, after the tourists have returned to their pricey rented rooms and the janitorial service workers start their fluorescent-lit jobs, after the streetlights and neon lights and car lights blot out any possibility of true darkness or star shine, after blaring city night street sounds make peace impossible, then it is time for Jim to set up his home on a Market Street sidewalk.

During the day, flanked by the shopping carts that hold everything he owns, Jim sits on a milk crate, holding court among his chosen friends. His most beloved and loyal friends are the Greek Orthodox icons that stare benevolently from the places where they are propped atop his carts. But there are other friends, too: Mickey (when he's sober and not feeling combative); Rafael, a young homeless artist; Big Jim, a former attorney on the verge of finding a place to live; Susan and Mark, what the city calls "a vehicularly housed" couple who pay their "rent" to daytime parking meters. The icon saints may pray for Jim, but these flesh-and-blood friends bring him food or guard his carts while he goes to stand in a line for food or mail or a toilet.

I met Jim one afternoon as he sat on a bench contemplating the varieties of pedestrians in United Nations Plaza. When I asked him if he'd like to have a neck and shoulder massage, he refused. He explained that he couldn't stand to be touched, saying simply, "I'm a Vietnam veteran, and when people get too close to me, I feel claustrophobic." So Jim and I talked instead. He emphasized words dramatically, in his Peruvian accent, with his tongue sometimes poking through the place where his front four teeth used to be. His trousers were dirty, his plaid flannel shirt had food stains on it, he was wearing a grungy baseball cap over his wavy gray hair, and he had sprinkled the insides of his shoes with baking soda to keep his feet dry.

After that first meeting, whenever I found Jim on the streets, he welcomed me and we talked again. I admired his intelligence, and he generously answered my questions about the nuances of street life. Much more hesitantly he shared a few details about his military service. Eventually those details

formed a mental collage, and the horror of Jim's Vietnam War experience became more real to me: the stench of the sweat and fear and adrenaline of four soldiers roasting inside an armored Patton tank for hours at a stretch, the knowledge that outside the tank an unseen enemy was eager to blow him into eternity, the images of the people he had killed—"too many people . . . soldiers, women, children . . . too many people."

Jim's "claustrophobia" is post-traumatic stress disorder. Veterans' Administration doctors prescribed a combination of five drugs that made him "feel like a zombie. I don't mind that it takes this away," Jim told me, pointing at his crotch. "That only gets me into trouble anyway. But when it takes this away," he said, pointing to his head, "I can't stand it." So usually he rejects the prescriptions. Instead he self-medicates with a mixture of bottled fruit punch and vodka, and an occasional toke of marijuana. The slow titration of chemicals throughout the hours helps to keep the worst of his memories at bay.

In due time Jim did begin to let me massage his neck and shoulders, and sometimes his hands. But he didn't allow my craft to get in the way of what was by then the essential for us: being present to each other. Slowly, gradually, Jim shared bits of his personal life before the war, and these details didn't at all match my first impression. For example, Jim speaks six languages ("seven if you count Latin"). And he holds two master's degrees, one from the University of California, Berkeley, and one from the Sorbonne in Paris. His heritage is Spanish and Greek, and he grew up on his father's Peruvian coffee plantation. Because the drug cartels surrounding the plantation were becoming increasingly violent, Jim was sent to France for his high school and college

educations. Regardless of how much of this is true (and, increasingly, I believe the majority of it to be), Jim is an articulate encyclopedia of information on everything from the Mayan peoples to jellyfish stings, from classical composers to how the dogmas of Greek and Roman Catholicism differ.

Almost daily, Jim attends Mass at the downtown Annunciation Greek Orthodox Cathedral. Once I made a tape of Russian liturgical music for him to play on the boom box he carried in his cart; on the cardboard insert of the tape's box I painstakingly listed the titles of the tracks and the English translations of the titles. Jim was thrilled with the music, but I needn't have bothered to write out the contents. He not only recognized and named each piece as soon as he heard it, but he also knew the entire sacred texts in Russian and English as well as in Latin and Greek!

In exchange for US citizenship, Jim enlisted in the US Army. After 'Nam, he was employed installing satellite antennas for the military. He lost that job when he began using cocaine to combat his flashbacks of the war. After he became homeless, he was more discriminating about his choice of drug. ("It's too dangerous out here, with as helpless as 'toot' [cocaine] leaves you," he explained. He is also discriminating about whom he lets into his life and whom he rebuffs; people of the streets seek him out for his wisdom, or to bum a cigarette from him, or just to be near him for the way things feel better within his orbit. Drunks, thieves, trouble-makers, and the heartless are generally not welcome, but gentle, harmless, caring folks can always find a place near Jim.

A natural mystic, Jim is on a first-name basis with the Holy Trinity and with the Virgin Mary. As a psychotic he struggles with depression and thoughts of suicide. If

mythologist Joseph Campbell was right—if a mystic can swim in the same waters that will drown a psychotic—Jim swims and drowns at the same time.

The sinking times happen when he feels cornered, threatened, and boxed in. That's when the flashbacks come, and he believes he's back in 'Nam again, fighting for his life. His mind blanks out. He can become terrifyingly strong and violent, "just like the military taught me." Once, he told me, he regained consciousness to find himself tied into a bed in the psychiatric ward of a hospital. He was informed that he had injured all three muggers who'd backed him to a wall, and after he had been subdued by several cops he'd "torn up a perfectly good ambulance" from the inside out. Jim hates the drowning times and will do anything not to be cornered, not to hurt others—anything, including sleeping outside and trying with all his skill to avoid conflict.

A much-folded-and-refolded piece of letterhead stationery, kept always in Jim's shirt pocket, proves that the kind manager of a downtown art supply store has given Jim permission to inhabit the space between the sidewalk and the recessed front door of the store at any time outside of business hours. This means that between seven p.m. and eight a.m., "home" for Jim is a luxurious sixteen-by-five-foot space flanked on three sides by recessed display windows, and on the fourth by the sidewalk of Market Street, the busiest artery in San Francisco. An awning that extends out over the sidewalk gives him further protection from rain and the ubiquitous flocks of downtown pigeons and seagulls.

After a year or so of seeing me almost every week, Jim has finally come to trust me enough to invite me to "come to my place after seven o'clock when the store closes." For a

non-street person, to be invited to a street camp, especially to Jim's digs, is a real honor, but the thought of being on the streets at night by myself makes me nervous.

Nevertheless, tonight I have shown up at Jim's place on Market Street at seven p.m. Jim is delighted; he welcomes me profusely and offers me a seat on a five-gallon pail topped with a pillow. From that perch I watch him and two of his friends go through the ritual of setting up his camp for the night. First they take brooms from Jim's carts and sweep away the day's accumulation of dirt, trash, spit, and cigarette butts from the sidewalk in front of the store and for a quarter of a block on either side of it. Then the homemaking begins. Twelve layers of tarps, sleeping bags, and blankets, all fastidiously aligned and always in the same order, become Jim's bed. His friends kid him about this compulsive formula, but no one messes with it. Overturned milk crates and five-gallon pails are strategically placed to become furniture. Three shopping carts are lined up along the sidewalk just inside his "property line." Turned upside down over the remainder of his possessions, then covered with tarps and bungee cords, the carts form a three-foot-high barrier to the street.

After all that is done, the best part of Jim's day begins. Homeless friends stop by in a steady stream. One friend has a part-time job cooking at the ballpark; he pulls from his backpack a stash of lukewarm Polish sausages and limp French fries. Another friend sits down and collapses in tears, telling us that his dog died this afternoon and that, having no place to bury it, he's had to wrap up his canine friend in a blanket and put it in a dumpster. Other friends come to share cigarettes or complaints or a bottle of cheap wine way past its "best before" date. A few people who don't have a place for

the night ask to stay. To one Jim says yes, to the others no. Among those gathered, philosophies are articulated, and wonderings, and sometimes prayers and arguments; love is spoken, and always sincerity, which, I have learned, can be different from truth-telling.

In a very short time that eighty square feet of storefront begins to feel like the best of worlds, abundant in all of life's necessities and many of its luxuries. I am reluctant to leave, except that I realize it's past midnight and my housemates have no idea where I am (though that's probably a good thing, considering where I actually am). For a while I have forgotten who I am, besides "Jim's friend," and I have forgotten where I belong, except "here," and I know no other people except these around me now. I am content; I feel fulfilled.

But this is an ephemeral world, one that will disappear with the return of morning light and the art store's business hours. Then Jim and a friend or two will pack it all up in the carts; from a nearby restaurant they'll bring out buckets of water to wash down the walls where passersby have pissed during the night; they'll leave the space cleaner than it was when Jim's entourage arrived. Then they'll make way for the store's customers and move down toward United Nations Plaza, where they may or may not be allowed to stay for the day.

❧

THE PROBLEM WITH DOORKNOBS

When I first started working on the streets of San Francisco, I learned to be so grateful for my own possessions, from my doorknobs to my 401(k) account. And that gratitude was a good thing. But then one day I heard

Father Richard Rohr talk about a poor man in Nairobi who, at the Prayers of the Faithful during a celebration of the Mass, prayed, "May we never live in stone houses." As I recall the story, after the service Father Rohr asked the man why he had asked God never to let him live in a stone house. The man replied that if you have a stone house, you can attach a doorframe in the opening, and if you have a doorframe, you can have a door hinged on. If you have a door, you will put your possessions behind that door so they will not be available to the others in your village. If you have your possessions behind the door, you will add a hasp and a latch and a lock to keep your possessions from the other villagers when you are away. And that is the beginning of the end of the life of your village. So it is better not ever to live in a stone house.

I began to look at my home—and my wonderful doorknobs—a little differently.

I wondered about the contrasts between what I had and what the street people had. I noticed that among many of them, despite how little they possessed, there was an innate, elusive sense of sufficiency, of enough-ness. Frustration, yes, at the restrictions imposed by their marginalization, and an inherent dissatisfaction with the compromised mental and physical health that had pushed them to the edges of society. And despair at how easily anything they own could be taken from them, stolen by others on the streets or confiscated by mandated "sweeps" of the places homeless people gather with their belongings. But still, many in the margins continued to look forward to what the next day would bring: playing chess with a buddy in the park, grilled-cheese-sandwich day at St. Anthony's Dining

Room, walking through the farmers' market and seeing the beauty of the produce and crafts in the stalls, going to the library for the next book in a mystery series.

But what if *enough* were redefined? How shall we speak realistically of deprivation and abundance in our world? How shall we draw a line between scarcity and sufficiency? Do we even want to know where that line is? The American government can discriminate statistically between poverty and excess in the United States—but there is no way that those definitions apply to refugee camps in sub-Saharan Africa. (One benchmark of poverty in the US is having an income of less than $32 USD per day. One benchmark of poverty in sub-Saharan Africa is having less than $1.25 USD per day.)

In his 1943 study of healthy people, Abraham Maslow posited a hierarchy of needs. The most basic of these are *deficiency needs*—the elements necessary for basic survival—and beyond this there are higher *being needs*: the ones that lead to a fuller, richer life.

In our social margins, where one can generally expect to get a daily allotment of food, water, air, sleep, and shelter, the definitions of *enough* stand in stark contrast with our cultural/commercial/consumer definitions of *enough*. And yet from the perspective of living in the margins, there is enough, and on some days there might be abundance.

I even came to recognize, in the people who became my teachers, aspects of the self-esteem and self-actualization that Maslow's colleagues put at the very tops of their pyramidal human fulfillment charts. Everywhere I went in the wide variety of social margins, I found pockets of happiness, creativity, gratitude, and generosity.

Not only do many people of the margins *have* enough—their *deficiency needs* are mostly met—but they also *are* enough. They know innately what Margaret Wheatley articulates in *Perseverance*:

> Discovering what lives deep inside us, as our natural condition, requires fearless curiosity . . . To investigate our interior, we have to trust that we're more than a collection of very bad things. We have to have faith that, at our core, we're essentially fine, whole, healthy. And we have to believe this about everyone, not just ourselves.

We *are* enough.

6

B EING E NOUGH :

D A Y E N U

*M*ore than a thousand years ago a Hebrew song became a part of the Jewish Passover celebration. This song repeats, many times over, the word *dayenu*, which translates as "it would have been enough for us." The meaning of the song is that any one of the gifts God gave to the Chosen People would have been enough, and yet another gift was given besides, and more beyond that.

I have experienced a subtle sense of *dayenu* among the people of our margins. From the *deficiency needs* there is food to share, or a cigarette, or a blanket. Furthermore, there is joy in the margins. There is goodness in the margins. And laughter, and generosity, and creativity, and wisdom. And there is sometimes *dayenu*: so much of the *being needs* that there is bounty to give away. There is enough creativity to shape small pockets of beauty. Some marginalized people have a sense of self-esteem strong enough to risk welcoming strangers. Some experience an abundance of being from which to interact with others who pause for a moment in the sphere of their lives.

People in the margins who have an underlying sense of *dayenu* have offered me opportunities to believe that I, too, am enough.

❧

Tea with Sandy

Her name is Sandy; she is a pretty woman with short-cropped hair the color of her name. She is forty, or maybe fifty, with a sunny smile and a graceful way of moving that makes her a pleasure to watch. She is clean and well groomed, and has a warm Texas accent. She would be unnoticed on the streets of San Francisco not because she is homeless and "unseeable," but because she'd fit right in with the workaday crowd and the shoppers. She makes eye contact easily, and the crinkles at the corners of her eyes speak of humor and hospitality. With that kind of openness, I guessed, when we first met, that she had not been on the streets long. I was mistaken.

"So, Sandy," I say, as I place a clean towel over the pillow on the desk at the center of the homeless shelter's women's dorm, "what can you tell me about your health? Any recent illnesses or broken bones?" She shakes her head. I probe further, "Any problems at all with your upper body?" My new-client "interviews" are general and informal, but necessary.

"No ma'am," she drawls. "Nothin' like that."

"Any cuts or bruises on your neck or shoulders or arms?"

"Nope. I'm in pretty good shape." She smiles brightly, sitting on a folding chair in front of the desk.

"Okay, then, let's get started."

I describe to her how we'll work together for the next twenty minutes, and just before she leans into the pillow, she says, "Maybe I should tell y'all, I do have this little brain tumor in my head, but it doesn't cause me much trouble."

*Dear God, **nothin'** but a little brain tumor!*

My hands pay particular attention to Sandy's neck and head, intending healing to go wherever her tumor might be.

It crosses my mind as I work: this could be me. This could be me. But my internal censor will not allow me to hold on to that thought for long. It is too fearsome.

Sandy basks in my touch. When we are finished, she slowly opens her eyes, looks straight into mine, and says softly, "Whooeee! Who are you? That was not just any old back rub! I'm gonna to be praying for you." We embrace. She thinks for a moment and then says, "I'm goin' back home tomorrow. Do you think y'all could visit me there some time, maybe do another massage?"

"In Texas?" I ask.

Her laughter sounds like wind chimes. "No!" she says. "My home out by the warehouse. Here, I'll draw you a map."

A few days later I am on my way home for the day and see nothing in front of me but a mess of tangled traffic trying to get to the Bay Bridge. On impulse I turn to the right, out of the gridlocked intersection I've been waiting to cross for the last five stoplight sequences. I dig out Sandy's map and decide to try to find her while the rush hour unsnarls itself.

I locate the area Sandy drew, a vacant two-acre field bordered by a four-hundred-foot-long warehouse on one side and a railroad spur on the opposite side; two rough gravel roadways complete the borders of the rectangular field. All I can see in the field, to which Sandy's penciled arrow points, are thick, seven-foot-high weeds that smell like licorice when I brush against them. I park in one of the gravel drives and walk along the railroad tracks, from one drive to the other. I must have misunderstood Sandy. There is

no hootch, no sign of life other than the weeds and a couple of gulls perched on the warehouse roof, arguing loudly about which one owns the remainder of a moldy hamburger.

I give up and head back toward my car. Then out of the corner of my eye, I notice a narrow space, barely twelve inches wide, opening into the weeds and disappearing immediately into the field. I look closer and step a few feet into the tall stalks; there is a path that makes a sharp right turn, then curves to the left. I follow it. Weeds brush on either side of me, weeds loom over my head, and walls of weeds rise before me and behind me. The oppressive closeness and the rich licorice smell make it difficult for me to breathe; the space is so narrow I begin to feel panicky, not wanting to move forward, yet afraid to turn around. Why have I come here alone, without a street partner? If fear paralyzes me here, how long will it take for someone to find me? Will a warehouse worker notice the gulls circling overhead and arguing over my moldy corpse? Just when I think I will scream from claustrophobia, the path opens out into a space several yards square, walled in by the weeds but open to the sky.

And there sits Sandy, smiling her welcome in front of her blue tarp home. She, of course, "heard somebody thrashin'" around on the way in." And with the street instincts that she has developed in her many years of homelessness, she was "pretty sure it was somebody safe, prob'ly you."

"Sandy, this is wonderful!" I say, in a flood of feeling that is as much relief at surviving suffocation as admiration for what Sandy has created. There are chairs, a cooking arrangement, five-gallon water containers, a cot deep under the tarp, wildflowers in a bottle on a cloth-draped table. "How long have you lived here?"

"Oh, about three years, I reckon," she says. Turns out she stays in shelters only when she is too sick from her cancer treatments to trust being outside on her own. Otherwise she lives here, hidden away from the world and the cops and everyone to whom she has not given an invitation and a map. "Y'all care for a cup of tea?"

For over an hour Sandy and I talk, sharing some of our life stories, exploring gently and equally the tender places that we both understand. I give her a seated massage as she basks in the sunlight. She shares a package of cookies.

And we laugh, oh how we laugh, so often and loud that I am afraid we'll betray the location of Sandy's secret home. This woman can switch accents instantly from Houston to London to New Delhi to the Bronx, and all in the same tale about the people she's met on the streets and in the medical institutions where she is treated. "So this nurse is sittin' beside me, and she's got this ol' rectal thermometer wedged on top of her ear. And I ask her, 'Why d'y'all have a rectal thermometer atop your ear?'

"She looks at me for a little bit, and she takes the thermo-meter off her ear, and her eyes go wide, and she says,"—and here Sandy switches into a perfect Latina accent—"'Uh-oh, I think I know where I left my pen!'"

Before I head back toward the Bay Bridge, Sandy and I stand and hold each other, sisters in an odd lineage that we have just now discovered. Then, like an unexpected barometric shift, the dregs of my laughter turn to tears; I don't want to leave. I have felt more at home in that isolated, destitute en-campment, and more enough in myself, than I could ever have predicted.

❧

THE QUALITIES OF ENOUGH-NESS

We know the general metrics of *having* enough—the basic level of physiological needs. But what can it mean to *be* enough? How can that be measured? What are its qualities?

I have no verbatim conversations to illustrate what I learned from the people of the margins about being enough, for no one there intended to teach anything of the sort. The learning was silent, wordless, and it rose within me as a result of my being present, stripped of all expectations, all intentions of service. Nevertheless, it's important that words be found, for this teaching is key to understanding how to see what has been made culturally invisible—it is this very enough-ness that we need to search for with our developing "marginal eyes."

For a while, as I was hunting for the right words, I carried a small notepad with me so that in a conversation I could catch words that I needed for my *enough* collection: *okay, accepted, loved, supported, seen, heart, holiness, resonance, happiness, gratitude, essence, reality, kinship.* There were pages of words and phrases that I snared, hoping to define the concept.

Often the words came from the realms of philosophy and theology. Of course, philosophy and theology are only approximations of the wisdom and divinity they study, and like any collections of words, like my collection of words, they always fall short of the reality.

It was important to me that the *enough* I hoped to pin down would not carry a sense of "just enough" or "only so much," as if *enough* required still more to be complete. This *enough* had to be, instead, an adequacy, a fullness at the center of things.

Finally I decided that this wordless idea of "being enough" is simply a tiny spark at the core of the humanity of each of us, whether we are in the margins or in the mainstream. Ram Dass says, in *Be Love Now*, "You will feel it in your own heart—not your physical heart or your emotional heart, but your spiritual heart, the place you point to in your chest when you say, 'I am.'"

It is a fragment of divinity.

No matter what form God takes for each of us—the benevolent bearded white man giving life to Adam on the ceiling of the Sistine Chapel; or the collection of exotic-named female deities; or the law-making, deal-making God of Abraham, forefather of Judaism, Christianity, and Islam; or the deva of the highest good in each of us—regardless of our chosen image, we all carry a piece of that divinity, that Source of our life, inside us. In many scriptures that Source has named itself I AM. In most theological discussions both words are capitalized, as is the tetragrammaton, YHWH. It is the mysterious something that sustains life within our bodies, and it is the mysterious something that leaves our bodies when we die. Whence it came, and where it goes, is speculation for other writing.

So long as life endures in a person, that spark, the fragment of divinity, glows. Perhaps when we die, it is extinguished. Perhaps, instead, when we die, it erupts into glorious flame. But in the meantime, in our lifetimes, when we notice the spark in each other, when we breathe on it, when we fan it with the motion of our own beating heart, the spark is enlivened. The spark of divinity, the God seed, the holy word in each of us is exactly the same as the name of God, the essence of God. The spark is not some

developed quality upon which others can pass social judgment. It is the very basis, the least common denominator of our mutual existence.

"I AM" is enough. There is no other quality that is needed. No further explanation, no other reason for existing, is required. Existing, *being*, is the core of life. "I AM." It is *enough*.

<center>❧</center>

Ritchie Peels an Apple

A man's dark shape fills the doorway; his bulk temporarily blocks the sunlight from the cavernous room. No one looks up, but everyone knows, by the change in light and the change in energy, that someone else has come into the shelter. Those in the room are people of the streets, and like creatures in a fearsome sea, they are exquisitely wary of the atmospheric changes that can mean life or death to them. Heartbeats measure a subtle pause, a communal breath held.

The new arrival walks into the gloom, closing the warehouse door behind him. His clothes are loose and filthy; his hair and beard are loose and filthy; even his skin is loose and filthy. Then the rest of them see it's just big old Ritchie, and their attention ratchets down a notch.

As his vision adjusts from the outside brightness, Ritchie can make out the forms of dozens of other homeless people—sitting; pacing; playing cards; wondering, now that lunch is over, how to kill time until supper. Can't go lie down—not unless you're sick and you've gotten permission and it's officially written down in the book. Can't turn on the TV—not allowed till seven o'clock at night. Can't take a shower

until two thirty. Already read the shelter's collection of books. Can't sit out on the front steps, or along the back of the building, or in the vacant lot next door—shelter "Guideline Number Six."

Ritchie has arrived too late for lunch. Two guys on the shelter staff, "livin' rough" themselves just last month, are already wiping down the tables, sweeping the floor, hauling out the garbage. There is a corrugated cardboard box on the counter with a few apples left in it; two of the apples disappear into Ritchie's pocket. He grabs a half-full milk carton from a garbage can and drinks it down.

Most of the tables in the room will be folded up to discourage leaning, lingering, or napping. But Ritchie spots a table where three guys have started a penny-ante poker game. The staff will probably let the game continue, and he heads for a chair at the end of that table. He ignores the poker players, and they ignore him.

The folding chair has seen many better days, and its seat slopes downward more than is comfortable, but it is a chair, and that's something; it's not too bad if you can slouch back and brace your feet on the floor. Ritchie sits, slouches back, and braces his feet. He rummages around in the left pocket of his coat and retrieves a gray plastic spoon. He pulls one of the apples from the right pocket. He settles himself into the work—the art—that will take up the next hour of his afternoon: consuming an apple.

First his thumbnail pierces the fruit, up near where the stem was. The apple was picked many months ago; its skin is nearly as tough as old Ritchie's ragged nail. A virgin apple, especially one this old, has to be pierced firmly. Then, carefully and expertly, his experienced fingers curl around to

support the flimsy bowl of his plastic spoon. The thin, leading edge of the spoon slides into the curved incision his nail has made; he pushes, just so, and a red sliver of the apple's skin falls to the scarred table. Another sliver follows, and then another.

All of Ritchie's ponderous attention is now on this apple and its peel. He leans down toward the table, tilting his chin to the right so his remaining eye, the left one, can spot the three pieces of peel. He finds them and deposits them in his empty milk carton. That done, he raises his head and pauses as if listening for something. He might be staring into the distance, except that now both of his eyelids are shut.

There is a prominent scar on the right side of his forehead, a smooth quarter-circle arc; its perfect geometry is a startling contrast to the imperfection below it. The right side of Ritchie's face sags fluidly, like a melting wax image. The outer corner of his right eyelid reaches down into the dark bags below the nonfunctioning eye, and those bags, in turn, sag toward the side of his mouth that doesn't move.

Ritchie pulls in a deep breath, sighs it out, and picks up his work again; his hazel-colored left eye opens several seconds later, as if the brain's message took longer to reach the eye than the hands. With determination, then, and surprising speed, the apple is denuded, its moist flesh totally exposed. He holds it up, slightly to the left, to inspect his work. It is now a small globe with evenly-spaced pock marks where the spoon dug deeper at the beginning of each stroke. He is unaware, or cares not, that his dirty fingers have turned the apple into a chronological grayscale—the portion of the apple last peeled is pale yellow, and each preceding portion is a slightly darker shade of grime.

All of the apple peel is piled into the milk carton now, and tiny chunks of carving debris are spread out over Ritchie's beard and belly. Another of the men walks by, says, "Hey, Ritchie, how ya doin'?" But this man doesn't really care how Ritchie's doing. The question is more a taunt than a greeting.

Ritchie moves his mouth as if responding, though no sounds emerge. His long, stringy gray hair and the left side of his face become expressive for a moment, as if Ritchie has hurled a brief obscenity at the other. But the epithet is silent, for Ritchie is mute, and that amuses the men who share the shelter with him.

Ritchie reverses the plastic spoon in his hand, holding the bowl of it in his palm and wielding the handle like a dagger. He stabs the belly of the apple. He rocks the spoon handle back and forth, widening the wound he's created. Gradually the fruit submits and splits in two. One half-apple falls and rocks on the table top beside the milk carton. He stabs at the piece that remains in his hand, trying to divide the half into quarters, but it shatters from the thrust. Patiently, Ritchie's old fingers gather up the fragments. He pokes them one at a time into the left side of his mouth, and chews with satisfaction.

Once more he sighs and stares out, or maybe in, at something only he can see. Slowly his left eye closes, and his breathing comes soft. His left hand had picked up the remaining apple half, to guard it; now both hands and the apple half rest on his belly, rising and falling with the regular rhythm of his breathing.

After a while Ritchie rouses. He pushes the milk carton just beyond the invisible boundaries of his tabletop turf. He

pulls a folded streamer of toilet paper from his right jacket pocket, detaches a length, wraps the uneaten apple half, and stashes it in the left pocket. Another length of toilet paper he wads up to begin cleaning the bits of apple and other detritus from his tangled beard. Methodically he finds it all. Cocking his head down to the left like a robin looking for worms, he wipes the crumbs from his belly and legs. Then he lifts a corner of his beard, and gently wipes out the hole in his throat where his voice used to be.

Ritchie stows the remaining wad of toilet paper. He carefully returns his precious plastic spoon to his left pocket, rises from his chair, and limps back out into the sunlit street.

༶

During the hour I just described, I was sitting with another street person across the room from Ritchie. It was my observation that during this entire episode, Ritchie was complete. He needed nothing given to him, he needed nothing fixed, he needed nothing changed. He was whole in himself. He was enough. *Dayenu.*

But what if there had been just one tiny element added that day? What if there had been a momentary acknowledgement of Ritchie's enough-ness? What if, for a moment, Ritchie had counted for something? What if there had been the briefest of deep eye contact, with just one other person, reflecting acceptance of Ritchie exactly as he is? What if Ritchie's shoulder had been touched, warmly, for two seconds? What if Ritchie had had a new awareness in his tired old bones that he was truly seen, and loved, just for being alive? No words, no expectations, nothing different except for one spark of divinity acknowledging

another spark of divinity. Would not both sparks have glowed a bit more brightly?

Dayenu—things as they were would have been enough, but then, unexpectedly, there might have been something more.

PART TWO:

Two Questions

Darest thou now, O Soul,
Walk out with me toward the Unknown Region,
Where neither ground is for the feet, nor any path to follow?

—Walt Whitman, *Leaves of Grass*

7

WHY GO THERE?

The margins, in their many varieties, can be scary places to be.

Hospitals are unnerving margins, filled with suffering and body fluids and antiseptic mysteries.

Slum streets are alarming margins, filled with unpredictable madness and poverty and addictions.

Prisons are intimidating margins, filled with angry felons.

Even next door may be a creepy margin, the darkened living room where an ancient person sits, isolated and rotting away.

Nursing homes are eerie margins, warehousing multiple ancient rotting persons.

Our cultural fringes comprise the vast detritus of our social and natural ailments—physical and mental and addiction illnesses, destitution, violence, and hatred, as well as racism, ageism, and all the other prejudicial *-isms* out of which we have fashioned our margins. Just considering the size of the margins makes me want to cower. I can't begin

to tackle all these problems; I can't even think about changing their causes. I'm overwhelmed by their sheer enormity.

"Let us not underestimate how hard it is to be compassionate," Henri J. M. Nouwen writes in *The Way of the Heart*. He continues:

> Compassion is hard because it requires the inner disposition to go with others to the place where they are weak, vulnerable, lonely, and broken. But this is not our spontaneous response to suffering. What we desire most is to do away with suffering by fleeing from it or finding a quick cure for it. . . . And so we ignore our greatest gift, which is our ability to enter into solidarity with those who suffer.

That's a nice sentiment on paper, but I repeat the question that is asked of me so often: Why would *anyone* ever deliberately go into the margins if they didn't have to?

It took me twenty years of being taught by the hidden teachers of the margins to be able to finally name four reasons why I go there, four reasons why anyone might consider going there:

To offer the intangible gifts that each of us has

To receive the intangible gifts that are offered in return

To carry precious stories from the periphery back to the mainstream where they need to be heard as the missing pieces of our communal story

Because we can

By ourselves, we can't correct the circumstances of the margins. And we may not feel able to bear the enormity of the collective misfortune that converges there.

But this we can do: we can cross the line that divides the middle from the margins.

And this we can do: we can choose to encounter one person at a time at the edges of our culture.

We can mutually offer and receive, and we can honor our encounters by carrying and sharing the stories of our "solidarity with those who suffer."

GO TO THE MARGINS TO OFFER

There are many things one can carry to the margins: clothes, food, medicine, money. But no matter how large or how small it is, a thing that is offered takes up space between a marginalized person and the giver—physical space, and psychological space. I believe it's better to go empty-handed, at least at first, and to offer only intangible gifts. Three of my favorites are marginal eyes, *wabi-sabi*, and physical touch.

Offer the Gift of Marginal Eyes

As my single most priceless intangible gift, I offer to an outcast my noticing, my "marginal eyes." What is mine to give is a presence that silently says, *You are seen. You are real. You are enough. You have a spark of divinity within you. That spark may be banked by suffering and hopelessness; that spark may be barely glowing. But my own spark flares when I notice yours. With my attention I will fan your fragment of divinity, to keep your ember alive.*

Everyone is instinctively, if unconsciously, aware of others' rejecting body language—the deliberately averted eyes, the shoulder turned slightly away, the downturned corners of a mouth, the suddenly busy actions that say, *No time for you.* "One of the greatest diseases is to be nobody to anybody," said Mother Teresa of Calcutta. We all crave other signals, assuring us that we are good, that we are worthy of notice, that we are enough: a smile, eye contact, a touch, a moment of sitting-with, a silence shared, a story heard.

❧

The Barefoot Cook

Martha is as much a fixture in the Tenderloin Café as the not-quite-level grill at which she works. Her arthritic feet are callused and bunioned and shoeless as she paces between the shelves of stacked plates, the eight-slice toaster, the piles of hamburger buns, and the tubs of condiments. Containers of eggs, two dozen in each, are stacked ten layers high to the right of the grill, and two deep-fat fryers bubble ominously to the left. At the far end of Martha's path is the chest freezer from which she pulls French-sliced potatoes or American-sliced potatoes, and chopped or sliced or breaded onions. The freezer's back edge rests on the floor at the upper slope of the café, and its front edge is propped up by two concrete blocks to keep it level.

I come to the Tenderloin Café about once a week for my favorite sandwich: grilled tuna salad. The secret to Martha's version of this sandwich is that the bread is toasted separately and the huge dollop of tuna-salad filling is flattened on the

grill and sautéed to a crispy brown on both sides; then everything is assembled with a little extra mayonnaise and lettuce leaves. Several times I have tried to duplicate this sandwich at home, and I always end up with a hopeless mess, so I have given up and just let Martha do it.

Martha limps as she hustles along her well-worn path behind the counter. An occasional sigh or quiet groan gives voice to the pain in her hips and knees and ankles as they complain about every ounce of her three hundred pounds. The adipose tissue in her arms and legs and belly wobbles as she prepares her customers' orders. She cooks for long stretches with just one scheduled half hour to rest at ten thirty, after the breakfast rush and before the lunch rush.

The Tenderloin Café isn't Martha's restaurant—she could never afford to buy or rent a coffee shop, even one with sloping floors in the Tenderloin. It has not been that many years since she lived in a homeless shelter. But she takes a proprietary interest in her boss's place because he gave her a chance at the job. She's never let him down, despite her daily pain. She doesn't talk much about that pain, and besides, as she says, "There are so many people here hurting worse than me; I got no cause to complain."

I try to arrive early so I can order my grilled tuna salad sandwich just before Martha's break time, when she will declare herself off duty. She sits down next to me at the upper end of the counter where she has a chair, more substantial than the patched stools the customers use. Sometimes we sit together in silence, but often she and I talk: "grandma talk," and gossip about the people of the streets, and complaints about City Hall, and opinions about the paperback books we've read most recently.

Sometimes we get around to stories about our own lives. She talks about her first husband, the love of her life, who died when he was thirty, hit by a drunk driver. I talk about my only husband, who loved me beyond measure and whom I learned to love well just a few years before he succumbed to heart failure. We talk less about her second husband, who could not deal with the hospital bills left over from her first husband's accident and who abandoned her and her teenage daughters; my son who was murdered at age thirteen; her daughter who was hooked on drugs. She doesn't talk at all about how she ended up on the streets, but that is implicit in the other tales. We don't tell the full stories, not the gory details, just enough to know the hurt places and to feel the compassion flowing between us. We can't fix each other, can't even really imagine the other's life. But we sit together at the high end of the counter, I eating my grilled tuna salad sandwich, Martha eating her cinnamon roll and a cup of coffee, and we listen. And we genuinely see each other.

❧

One who is invisible is never seen, doesn't exist to anyone else. But what happens when they are offered the gift of attention and curiosity—not idle nosiness, but an honest wondering? *Who are you truly? Who am I when I am with you? What might we say to each other if we took the chance? What would happen if our encounter temporarily softened the hard edges of our lives?* What if we saw, and had compassion for, our mutual brokenness? The gift of marginal eyes is priceless, in the margins, in our homes, at work—wherever it is offered.

Offer the Gift of *Wabi-Sabi*

We can bring to the margins an appreciation for what the Japanese call *wabi-sabi*—the beauty of imperfection. *Wabi-sabi* is a spiritual aesthetic, an acknowledgement that everything is incomplete, everything is imperfect, everything is impermanent. In the Buddhist view these are good qualities, leading to a simpler life and even transcendence. The chorus to Leonard Cohen's song "Anthem" advises, "Forget your perfect offering / There is a crack in everything / That's how the light gets in."

In my view, the *wabi-sabi* of human embodiment—frailty, longing, awkward repairs in the broken places of our biographies—causes me to smile in recognition of what I know, and hope eventually to love, about myself. *Wabi-sabi* is a condition of being enough, of being a flawed human container for the small but perfect God-seed. My own *wabi-sabi* nods in recognition of my kinship with the *wabi-sabi* in my neighbor.

❧

The Prostitute and the Beautiful Man

Harry lies dead on a gurney a few yards away in emergency room cubicle 2. Ruth, his wife-now-widow, stands up, turns, and storms out of my cramped chaplain's office, heading for the sliding glass doors of the emergency room entrance. I follow a few paces behind, but she never looks back. She is angry, and afraid, and devastated. She has (correctly) guessed the circumstances of her husband's death—he had a heart attack in the arms of a prostitute at Saigon Spa.

As Ruth disappears into the darkness of the parking lot, I pause, thinking about all the pieces of the puzzle that Ruth had not needed in order to make the intuitive leap to the picture of Harry's death scene.

Then, like a puzzle piece retrieved from the polished marble floor, a small Asian woman materializes in the entryway. She looks lost and scared, and my mind makes an intuitive leap of its own. "May I help you?" I ask. I can guess who she is, but why has she come here?

"I look for Harry," she says. "He very sick."

"Come with me," I say. "We can sit over here to talk."

She is lovely, with fine features and clear eyes, and an appealing vulnerability that must be an asset in her trade among men who are used to harder, tougher whores.

"The man you are looking for—Harry—he was with you tonight? And he got sick while he was with you?" I ask.

"Yes," she says, unsure whether to be glad or to be wary that I might understand who she is. "They take him. They tell me this hospital."

"Would you tell me your name?" I ask.

"Rose," she says. Probably her professional name.

"Rose, may I ask why you've come here?"

"To see Harry," she says simply. "To see he okay. He nice man. Gentle. Talk nice. He laugh, and I laugh. I want to see he okay."

"Rose, Harry has died. He had a heart attack. The doctors worked hard to save him, but they couldn't get his heart to start again."

Her expression does not change, and she does not take her eyes from mine—she's learned how to do that in America —but trickles of tears begin to wander down her face. She

takes a deep breath, absorbing the information. "He so beautiful. Now his heart dead. Harry dead. He with me, and . . . oh!" She looks down, suddenly frightened.

"Rose, it's not your fault. You're not responsible. He had something wrong with his heart. It could have happened anytime, anywhere."

She studies her hands for a while, then makes up her mind. Quietly, courageously, she asks, "I come to see Harry. May I see Harry?"

Several layers of hospital regulations and policies say, "No."

But I say, "Over this way, Rose." It is always easier to ask forgiveness than to ask permission in an institution.

I nod to the guard at the waiting room desk, and without question he pushes the button that allows us back into the treatment area. I take Rose to cubicle 2 and pull the curtain closed behind us. She moves to the dead man's side. "He beautiful," she says again, and now, as she says it, I, too, can see his beauty. She touches his final day's growth of whiskers, runs two small fingers across his cheek and chin. "I'm sorry you die," she says to him. "Goodbye, Harry."

"Thank you," she says quietly to me. Like the medical staff, she has now done all she can.

As I walk Rose back to the night beyond the sliding glass doors, I thank her for her concern, for her tenderness. "How long had you and Harry known each other?" I ask, hoping not to sound impertinent.

At first she doesn't understand my question. Then she says, "Oh, I not know Harry. Just tonight. I meet him only tonight. First time he visit me. He beautiful."

She looks into the street-lit distance, then walks away, a

single asymmetrical human puzzle piece returning to the jumble of the unassembled wabi-sabi *picture.*

༄

Offer the Gift of Physical Touch

A *Wall Street Journal* article on March 13, 2012, touted the "tangible health benefits" of massage, which included a reduction in the stress hormone cortisol, a decrease in proteins related to inflammation and allergic reactions, and increased white blood cells that fight infection. A 2008 study published in the *Annals of Internal Medicine* comparing massage with simple touch for patients with advanced cancer found that simple touch "appears to have had a beneficial effect over time similar to that of massage," and recommends that "the potential benefits of attention and simple touch should . . . be considered."

Although some training helps to bestow confidence to the giver of this gift, one need not be a certified massage therapist in order to offer the comfort of touch. Marginalized people are perpetually touch-deprived, and simple touch is an easily portable present that can be offered as a sign of connection and inclusion in the human family. This gift must be offered respectfully: don't assume that it is okay. Ask, "May I put my hand on your arm?" Offering is gracious; touching for more than a few seconds without asking is presumptuous and rude.

A stranger in the margins should be touched not on their trunk but on their extremities—forearms, shoulders, perhaps knees if you're both sitting—and at first only on clothed or covered areas. Watch the person's face and end

the touch immediately if there are signs of discomfort. If it seems appropriate and you have permission, you might hold a hand or touch an arm skin-to-skin. And how would it be if, when you hand a dollar bill out your car window to the panhandler at the stoplight, your fingers linger for an instant on his hand, connecting one needy human heart to another?

I understand that touch is abused in our society, and some of the proscriptions against inappropriate touch are warranted. But I can't help but wonder: Would we have a different perspective, would we all feel more nurtured if we actually touched one another during the day?

My best friend, Chris, came from Michigan to Berkeley on a fact-finding mission disguised as a short vacation. It had been three years since I'd left Grand Rapids. Chris (and my family, and the hospital where I'd served as chaplain) had expected me to return there at least a year before, when I completed the master's degree that was the whole point of my coming to California. But I was showing no signs of budging in an eastward direction. So she brought herself west to investigate whether I'd finally lost my mind with all this "street work" stuff I talked about.

I took Chris to see the highlights of San Francisco. We marveled at the murals in the Mission District; we corkscrewed down Lombard Street; we passed beneath the orange towers and cables of the Golden Gate Bridge; we hiked and picnicked on Mt. Tamalpais. Every once in a while I showed Chris some of the places where I worked, and some of the invisible people that she'd not noticed until I pointed them out under a viaduct, deep in an alleyway, in

the shrubs of Golden Gate Park, or lying hidden under a sheet of corrugated cardboard on a sidewalk.

On the third night of her stay, I asked Chris if she'd like to go with me the next day to meet some of the people of the streets. I could tell that her heart stopped for the briefest of moments, and then she gamely said, "Sure."

"Okay, then, I'm going to give you my personalized crash course in street massage."

Her eyes widened in alarm. "You mean you're gonna want me to do massage?"

"Yup, kibitzing's not allowed."

That evening I created a very abbreviated version of the hand and arm massage that I sometimes taught for the Care Through Touch Institute. I massaged Chris's hand and showed her how it feels to have the bones and knuckles of the hand acknowledged with gentle squeezing and stroking; how lovely it feels to have someone else's fingers trace the long tendons that reach from the wrist to the base of the fingers; and the location of the sweet space that lies between the two bones of the forearm where the muscles just beg to be kneaded. Then I had her massage my hands while I coached her to "slow down," or to stroke "all the way past the wrist into the forearm."

My impromptu plans for the next day would not have been approved by my mentor, Mary Ann. There were two things about our work on which she and I did not exactly agree. We had "philosophical discussions" about who exclusively should receive Care Through Touch massage. She said it should be only our most destitute citizens, those who are otherwise never touched except in violence. I said that even the CEO with a corner office on the twenty-third floor

of a downtown building has a need to be touched with compassion. And we agreed to disagree about who was qualified to offer street massage: She said she would approve only those who had been through a Care Through Touch street-massage training, even if they were already certified as a massage therapist. I said that two hours of skill-learning was preparation enough for anyone with compassionate intention.

The next day's trip into San Francisco would be another opportunity for me to employ my easier-forgiveness-than-permission philosophy. With her open heart and her love of sensuous touch, I was sure Chris would prove herself worthy of my trust and the trust of those she would encounter. I could think of no better way to help her understand why I hadn't returned to Michigan than to have her experience this amazing work with her own hands, see it with her own eyes. As a bonus, my reliable street partner Dale had agreed to go with us and keep watch over us, and not to "snitch" on us until after the fact.

❦

Chris Improvises

The first people we approach this morning are three twenty-something men hanging out with a boom box on a bench near downtown. They assume various poses of disinterest, though they watch every step we take, trying to find a likely category with which to label us before we reach them. Dale introduces Chris and me, tells them what we are there for, and asks if they would like to have a hand massage. The first man, shoulders hunched indifferently under a brown scarf, hands

in jeans pockets, says, "Nah, that's not for me," gets up off the bench, and ambles away.

The second, wearing a dark gray hoodie that hides half his face, says, "I had one of these before. Would you massage my shoulders?" That will have to be me, because Chris hasn't learned that part.

The third man stays too. He has an impressive set of dreadlocks and lots of ear and eyebrow piercings. Chris bravely approaches him, racking her brain to remember what she is supposed to say or do next. That's when I see what I haven't noticed till now: the man's right forearm is in a blue fiberglass cast, hidden earlier under the blue jacket laid across his lap, and the cast runs from just below his elbow to the base of his fingers! This was definitely not in the curriculum of what Chris learned last night. But I already have my hands resting on the shoulders of the man in the gray hoodie, and will not interrupt what I have begun. I focus all my attention on the story beneath my own hands, and Chris is on her own.

I was right about her—Chris is a natural. The man with the dreadlocks and the piercings and the cast—his name is Greg—is moved by her work. (Later she tells me that she massaged his left arm and hand first, taking her time, feeling for more than the physical connection between them. By the time she had finished with that arm she was ready to improvise with the damaged arm. She stroked the exposed fingers on that right side, careful not to move them too much. Then for a long while she just held the cast gently between both of her palms as if she could feel, and he could feel, the warmth of contact between them. "Was that okay?" she asked me. It was more than okay.)

I have completed the shoulder massage for Howie, the man in the hoodie. I move around to the front of the bench and sit next to him; he and I silently watch Chris and Greg. Now that Chris has finished her work, she sits on the grass, scanning Greg's relaxed face, waiting for him to open his eyes. Even before he looks at her, he speaks, in an attractive Caribbean accent, saying, "I will nevah forget you."

Chris grins, knowing that probably he uses that line often—and knowing, too, that it might be true, and that she certainly will never forget Greg and the compassionate touch she has given him.

❧

Well-intentioned heart energy that flows into gentle touch can leave a glow of recognition and self-esteem that lasts for hours in someone who hasn't experienced physical contact in months.

And . . . "it's reciprocal."

GO TO THE MARGINS TO RECEIVE

The people of our social borderlands don't intend to gift others from their elemental enough-ness. The marginalized don't expect others to benefit simply from being in their presence. Few can conceive that they have any value at all, and if you pointed out to them that their presence is a gift, they would not believe you.

There are, however, many gifts waiting to be received from those in the margins.

Cynthia Trenshaw

Receive the Gift of Synergy

Sometimes something surprising happens when two people come together—an unexpected something that is unpredictable from the actions of either person alone. In *Synergetics*, systems theorist Buckminster Fuller coined a word for this: An "unpredicted, only-mutual behavior is *synergy*. *Synergy* is the only word in any language having this meaning." My friend Chris may have gone to the streets expecting to feel frightened, or charitable, or out of her element. Greg, the homeless man, may have expected to feel patronized or foolish for accepting a massage. But the synergy of their encounter created something new for each of them.

In the hours after Chris gave hand massages on the streets, over and over again she used the word *honored*. "I felt so honored that he allowed me to touch him. . . . I was in a 'bubble' where everything else disappeared around us. I felt privileged that he and I were brought together and protected like that. It felt . . . spiritual." Chris and Greg each went back to their respective milieus, but after their encounter both of them carried an unpredictable something: a sense of mutual respect that raised their appreciation of themselves and of humankind just a speck. It happened in a way that neither could have anticipated nor articulated. That particular speck of "better" in the world would not have happened with any other two people, and could not have happened at all if they had not come together and allowed their hearts to open to those moments. Brennan Manning writes in *Abba's Child*, "Our hearts of stone become hearts of flesh when we learn where the outcast weeps." That is a synergy of the margins.

❧

Chris and the Bag Lady

Years later the result of that episode of synergy is still affecting Chris's life.

She says, "Even now I look at street people differently. The other day, near the downtown library, a bag lady approached me. She asked if I had some aspirins that she might have. She wasn't scamming me. She didn't offer a complicated story or ask for money. It was a simple request, a simple need. I didn't have aspirins or any other pain medicine with me. But I took the time to tell her my name. And I asked what her name was. She said it was Gwen. Somehow the sharing of our names changed her from a 'bag lady' into a whole person in my eyes." For a moment Gwen was whole and Chris was whole.

And in their exchange each of them was a bit more than that: a tiny gift of healing to the world.

Synergy.

❧

Receive the Gift of Transcending Our Comfort Zone

The margins are teeming with unabridged, unedited, undiluted life and raw need. I want to have the courage to see it all, not avert my eyes. I acknowledge—and am profoundly grateful—that I can also leave most of the margins I enter. I can return to the comfort and security of my life in the middle. But I believe that I was given life in order to experience the human condition as fully as I can.

The margins are an enormous chunk of experience that has been excised from our society. I want to take the risk of going there.

There are no guarantees about going to the margins. It's possible that when I go, there will be nothing for me there but rejection, fear, and ugliness. That rarely happens, but when it does, I realize that, if nothing else, I have come to terms with a new piece of my own vulnerability or fear or even arrogance. If my fear and hubris reject something from my life, I can never experience that thing. What I open myself to, what I risk, what I welcome, even if I am not welcomed in return, widens my heart and enlivens my day.

"You have to go to the places that scare you so that you can see: What do you really believe?" Alice Walker writes. "Who are you really? Are you prepared to take this all the way to wherever the truth leads you and accept that you have to figure out different ways of confronting reality?"

❧

The Man on the Mattress

Carol, my street partner today, is driving and I've been talking, so I'm not certain where in the city we are—somewhere south of Cesar Chavez Street, I think. We are surrounded by warehouses and commercial buildings. There is a brightly painted taco wagon parked in the middle of the block, from which we have just bought what Carol says are excellent fish tacos. This is the first time I have tasted horchata, a milky sweet Spanish drink of ground almonds and vanilla. But what I will remember most clearly about today is the man on the mattress.

Across from the taco wagon, Carol and I sit on a low rock wall to eat our lunch. The wall divides the sidewalk from a little pocket park, only about forty feet square and filled with scraggly bushes and two decrepit benches at the end farthest from where we sit. The bushes are thick behind us, and we can't see through them from where we are. But when Carol looks down at the base of the bushes she notices red hypodermic needle caps in the dirt. "I wonder," she says, as she gets up and finds a way around the bushes.

I don't wonder, and I don't want to find what has been in those pieces of plastic. I have no affection for hypodermic needles, nor am I particularly interested in who might now have the needles that came in the discarded red caps. I just want to eat my fish tacos. I argue with myself for a while, but then reluctantly follow where Carol has gone.

When I catch up with her, she is talking with a group of four men who are shooting up their drug of choice. She is assuring them that we are cool with what they are doing, that we are massage therapists working with street folks to try to bring some comfort to them. And they are assuring her that they have all the comfort they need in the elastic tourniquets and the needles that have already found their raised veins.

I haven't passed out, but I do flinch away, and in doing so I notice a pile of something on the ground in the corner of the park. Crammed into an angle of cyclone fencing is an old mattress with huge scorch marks and one corner burned away. The fabric is soaked from an earlier rain, and it is rank with smoke and urine. But a man lies on the mattress, curled up like a child, with his wadded jacket pillowing his head. He is nearly unconscious and he has track marks on the arm that is crooked up toward his head. I squat down beside

*the mattress and watch him for a moment; when I see that he
is breathing, I ask if he is okay.*

"Oh yeah," he says, with a wobbly smile.

*And though I am in a place way beyond my comfort
zone, I feel somehow safe, and inexplicably linked with this
drugged homeless man. He has been stripped of everything
but his tenuous hold on life. I do not know his name. As I sit
with him I, too, am stripped to the basics: no name, no
position, none of the symbols of my status. We are two specks
of humbled humanity, each seeking just the next breath, just
the next heartbeat, in the margins. That's all there is for
now, and for now it must be enough.*

I hold his hand while he falls asleep.

❧

Receive the Gift of Hurt That Is Not Harm

Seeing what is daily in front of me is far different from
deliberately heading toward the margins.

Noticing what happens to cross my path is different
from deliberately seeking out what may cause me to squirm
in discomfort.

After my initiation into street work, I worried that I
would be harmed by the intensity of raw, uncamouflaged
life in those margins. And it was true that often what I saw
was hurtful to me. I experienced an empathic pain, an
anguish because I was unable to change things or make life
better for others. But never did that hurt actually harm me.

On the contrary, sometimes my "broken heart" became
the very opening through which I wanted to walk but
hadn't known how to find.

I couldn't have survived in chaplaincy or street work or years of personal caregiving if I hadn't learned the difference between discomfort and damage, if I hadn't learned that not everything that causes hurt causes harm.

In a strenuous physical workout, discomfort can be a symptom that you are exactly where you should be. Pain is not the goal but, rather, a sign that you're on the path to that goal. There is a saying about physical fitness: *No pain, no gain.* It is not literally true, for when exercise is taken to the point of actual pain, small rips in muscle fibers and fascia can undo any gains in strength. But the real meaning of the phrase is that if you don't move to and just slightly beyond the threshold where comfort and discomfort meet, you will not make any progress. Similarly, like the high after a good physical workout, the gifts found in the margins are often worth whatever discomfort it costs to receive them. This is what a certain renegade priest calls "costly grace."

In San Francisco's Polk Street neighborhood, Father River Sims's workday begins around eight p.m. and ends when he is too exhausted to continue. When I met him in 1998, River was in his early forties, a former Methodist minister and former prostitute. By the time our paths crossed, he had been ordained a priest of the Evangelical Anglican Church in America and was founder of Temenos Catholic Worker, an agency that he ran (and as of this writing, still runs) almost single-handedly.

Like members of the Catholic Worker movement after which he models his work, River is committed to voluntary poverty and direct service to social outcasts. He says that in ancient Greece, the *temenos* was an area outside the city walls, cut off from more respectable citizens, to which

prostitutes and other marginalized people were relegated.

River calls himself an "outlaw priest." On the streets during the night and at a large second-story flat during the day, River ministers around the clock to homeless teens who are runaways, throwaways, sex workers, and drug addicts. He subscribes to a philosophy of "radical harm reduction," which means that while he doesn't condone illegal drugs and dangerous lifestyles, he seeks to reduce the harms caused by them. So he exchanges new "points" for the blunted used needles that can scar veins and cause infections. He provides the condoms and lubricants needed for safe sex.

On the street, carrying his two huge signature gym bags with their straps crossed over his chest, he lugs hundreds of needles ("longs or shorts?") to exchange, hundreds of condoms to hand out, dozens of sandwiches that he spends hours making, clean socks and T-shirts and first aid materials. At eight p.m. those bags must weigh thirty pounds each; by four a.m. they weigh nothing, and River heads to his own tiny apartment for a few hours' sleep before beginning the work all over again.

At the Temenos flat he offers blankets and food and a few hours of respite from the rigors and terrors of the sex trade. The walls of the high-ceilinged apartment over-looking the street are filled with paintings and drawings and writings made by the young people. The room is crowded with tables and chairs, electric pots filled with soup, stacks of sandwiches, boxes of art supplies. Here the teens of the Polk Street neighborhood can get a stash of condoms and lubricant; they can exchange used needles for clean ones, grab a peanut butter and jelly sandwich, express themselves

in pastels or watercolors, talk about safe sex or stupid johns. They can attend daily Mass, come in out of the rain, get advice on how to avoid being arrested, and on some days, when Care Through Touch volunteers are there, they can get a chair massage.

❧

"Hare"

Hare has a red tattoo of an elongated rabbit running around his upper left arm, about where he places his tourniquet for drug injections. "Hare" is short for Harrison, a name he despises, but he likes the shorter version and has adopted the hare as his totem. He's been on the streets for two years since running away at fourteen from an abusive home in Omaha. His family never bothered to report him missing. He has shoulder-length black hair and stunning blue eyes, a pretty Irish boy who sells his body daily to earn enough money for his drug habit—"the rabbit's habit," he says, "the hare's heroin," smiling at his well-worn clever phrases.

Hare tells me he'd like to have a back massage—he didn't sleep well on the pavement in the early hours of this morning, after his tricks were finished, and his muscles are sore. He pulls a folding chair up to one of the long tables in the big room, and I place a pillow in front of him and explain how he should lean into the pillow, and what he might expect from the massage. What I can't explain, what I couldn't have predicted, is how the experience will devastate me.

As soon as Hare begins to relax under my hands, I feel something I've never felt so intensely before—a tingling, like an irregular low-voltage electrical current. I don't know for

*certain what it is and couldn't swear that I actually feel it,
but the image that comes to me is that of a small generator
shorting out, emitting aberrant bursts of power. It feels as if
this young healthy body is struggling to live in spite of all the
ways Hare is trying to kill it, and it is the most heartbreaking
message I've ever received from a body. I weep for the waste
of it all. After twenty minutes, my brimming eyes make my
hands look hazy as they gently touch down on Hare's head in
the final blessing of his massage. Then I silently bow to his
confused, resting body, and go to the window to stare down
at the street for a long, long time.*

*Feeling the terrible pain of Hare's life, I wonder why—and
how—River keeps on serving these kids. He can give a hundred
answers, many of them having to do with the example set by
Jesus working in the margins of His own culture. Some of his
reasons have to do with hope: "I give the teenagers the means
to survive until they someday, maybe, reach the point of wanting
to make different choices." He is realistic about how unlikely
that is, and continuously the reality hurts. Yet there have been
those rare moments when one of the teens has understood
unconditional love, when the light has come back on behind
their eyes, and they have felt hope. Over the years there have
even been a few teens salvaged from the drugs and the street life.*

*While many would call River crazy—most saints have
been so labeled in their lifetimes—there is an odd kind of joy
in his work. He acknowledges the spiritual quandary: this
kind of intense work, he says, is "costly grace," and he feels
the cost, and the grace, daily.*

*I marveled briefly at both sides of that equation as I
massaged Hare. It is a holy paradox: the gift of hurt that does*

not harm. Scary to face, difficult to continue to believe in, impossible to ignore when experienced. It meets us where life is lived in its most elemental, undiluted, undisguised form: at the edge, in the margins.

❧

GO TO THE MARGINS TO CARRY BACK STORIES

"It is the experiences you share with others and the stories that you tell about those experiences afterward, and the tales you bring from the past and future, that create the ultimate bond," writes Clarissa Pinkola Estés. In her tiny book *The Gift of Story: A Wise Tale About What Is Enough,* Estés tells of Bal Shem Tov, founder of Hasidic Judaism. As the great spiritual leader of his people, Estes says, Bal Shem Tov knew the sacred place in the forest, knew how to light the fire, and knew how to say the prayer. And because of this, God always came to the people. It is said that after Bal Shem Tov's death, the generations of his followers gradually forgot the location of the special place; then they forgot how to light the fire, but they remembered the prayer and God still came. Eventually they forgot how to say the prayer. "But one person still remembered the story about it all, and told it aloud. And God still came." Estés says that "[when] at least one soul remains who can tell the story . . . by the recounting of the tale, the greater forces of love, mercy, generosity and strength are continuously called into being in the world."

Whatever it was that ripped a person gradually or precipitously away to the margins has caused them to lose their say, to lose the story of who they thought they were.

How do they recover their story, or create a new story, when everything in the margins—the streets, the shelters, the agencies, the hospitals, the caregivers, the mortgage broker, the unemployment office, the divorce decree—erodes their sense of self? Who can look deeper, beneath the marginal labels, to help them to find a more real story?

There is no place in the world where life is more intense, where the stories are more condensed and more real, than in the margins of a culture. Might we approach a person there with two types of wonder: a sense of curiosity (Who are you? What may I learn from you?) and a sense of awe (for the person, for the God-seed, for the absolutely unique story that belongs to this person)? Can we be amazed that we are the only person in all the world to have arrived in this place, at this exact time, in order to witness this moment in the life of this particular person? Can we have the patience to listen to, to honor, and then reverently to hold this precious story? Can we carry this story back to the hub of the circle, the sacred place of our community, where we build our fires and rest our prayers? Can we return a fragment of the margins back to the heart of the family from which it was lost?

Carrying the stories back across the border, from the lost part of our community to those who were not aware anyone had gone missing, is like sewing up a cultural gash one stitch at a time. Each encounter carried and shared reattaches a scrap of our disconnected kin to the lovely, tattered, patched-together human family quilt.

If necessary, think of forays into the margins as a form of self-preservation: it is the story carriers who are invited closest to the warmth of the communal fire. Think of your

courage as insurance against a time when you become more marginalized (as inevitably you will, merely by growing older, poorer, frailer, closer to dying). It is the compassionate listeners and the tellers of the essential human stories who most easily cross our cultural lines in both directions and who smudge and soften, if not eliminate, the edges of the margins.

GO TO THE MARGINS BECAUSE YOU CAN

We are programmed for community, for being with one another. Our lives are enriched by deliberately meeting with others, different others, to broaden our sense of the human condition. When we choose to do so, we can extend our human family and our connections within that family. We can cross paths, like one woolen thread crossing another, enriching the tapestry of the human story. We who have the mobility of citizens of the middle are like travelers with universal passports. We can cross the boundaries of the margins whenever we wish, expanding the limits of our community to include those who hunger to belong.

Our "universal passports" assure that once we have crossed the boundary, we are not stuck permanently in the fringes. At least until our "passports" expire, we can also easily return to the middle. But this is a *why go there* reason that is not always reciprocal—the borders are not equally permeable from the outside in. If the social wastelands are eventually to be lessened on our community maps, it will be through the initiative of community presence being extended from the center to the edges. It will be through invitations to come to the middle, through ordinary citizens

reconnecting with our outcasts one encounter at a time and inviting them to come, escorting them to sit around the warmth of the fire—if they choose.

❧

Oh, the Places We'll Go . . . or Not

Imagine a woman's broad-brimmed straw hat decorated with green ribbon and white silk daisies. Imagine it sitting atop a bright ball of light that moves eagerly through the Tenderloin, seeking, shining on whatever beauty it can find, bringing unexpected brightness to dark corners. Now gradually let that image morph into a perky black woman, her head covered with tight, ribboned cornrows beneath her signature flowered hat. She has eyes that sparkle and a smile that just won't quit. That's Joyce, a jaunty force of nature in perpetual motion.

Joyce was a patient at San Francisco's multi-service clinic named after Olympic athlete Dr. Tom Waddell. I volunteered at the clinic once a week, offering alternative therapies (craniosacral, shiatsu, massage) to patients. When her healthcare worker recommended craniosacral therapy, Joyce jumped at the chance to experience something new. I was immediately charmed by her. That was pretty much everyone's response to Joyce. She had lots of physical problems, among them spastic vocal cords that made her speech much more quiet than her personality. In her whispery voice she proclaimed joyfully, "Nobody, no-body, is a stranger to me."

I saw Joyce weekly for a few months, and was energized by her enthusiasm for living and learning. One day we were talking about stars; spontaneously, I asked her if she'd like to come to Oakland to see one of the shows at the Chabot Space

Center Planetarium. "I can pick you up, and we can have lunch, and then we can see the show. The planetarium is just a few miles from where I live."

The plans were made, and her excitement grew as we got nearer to the date, but when the day came and I arrived at the place where I was to meet her, Joyce was not there. I waited for an hour, and she did not show up. The next week, when she came in for a session, she told me, "I just couldn't do it. I just couldn't." And her eyes begged for my understanding.

The line demarcating the margins from the middle was an invisible electric fence against which Joyce had been zapped so many times that she was now fully "trained" to remain on "her" side. So if she and I were to continue our joyful, enriching interactions, it would have to be me who continued to come to her. Until maybe someday . . .

೧

In his challenging book *The Careless Society*, written in 1994 and still often required reading for social services students, Northwestern University professor John McKnight describes the propensity for social labeling in our culture. Labeling is the process of focusing on deficiencies rather than abilities. These labeled deficiencies, such as *mentally disabled* or *homeless* or *physically disabled* or *disadvantaged* or *aged* or *destitute*, probably cannot be fixed. Yet the assertion that they should be corrected undergirds the whole of our social services system. Furthermore, McKnight argues, a system that focuses on deficiencies fails to focus on the capacities of those same labeled people. The system persuades the citizens of the community that these vulnerable people "cannot be incorporated into community life because

citizens don't know how to deal with these special people."

The system is mistaken. We community citizens are needed in all the margins of our society—not just in the streets with their homeless people, which are arguably our most formidable margins, but also in those hidden margins of the housed, the labeled ones who inhabit hospital corridors, nursing homes, group homes, orphanages, and private homes. McKnight writes:

> For those whose "emptiness" cannot be filled by human services the most obvious "need" is the opportunity to express and share their gifts, skills, capacities, and abilities with friends, neighbors, and fellow citizens in the community.

I've experienced the intangible gifts ordinary citizens have to offer to those cut off by social labeling.

I've experienced the intangible gifts that the isolated, vulnerable people of the margins have to offer in return.

And I'm convinced that we certainly *do* "know how to deal with these special people." Furthermore, if we hope to heal our wounded society, it is our obligation—and perhaps our joy—to do so.

Later in this book I will tell the story of a woman who had had an amputation years before but still felt pain where the missing part of her body had been. That's the way I sometimes see our culture: huge chunks have been amputated, and we feel a shadowy pain, an unidentifiable social malaise, where the parts should still be. If we happen to catch sight of the amputated "parts"—sleeping on sidewalks or lying in nursing homes or trying to sell themselves for sex—our discomfort increases. Though we

tend to experience this pain as revulsion or anger or judgment rather than longing, I believe it is a recognition that something enormous is missing from our community.

The psychologist C. G. Jung writes about our "shadow aspect," which contains everything of which we are not consciously aware. That includes things positive as well as negative: if we ignore the shadow, we miss out on both. The more we become conscious of the margins—our culture's storage space for the people we've cut off from ourselves—the more we come to terms with not only the negative in that storage space (mental, physical, and addictive illnesses; mortality; shattered lives) but also the positive that is hiding in there as well (kinship, gratitude, creativity, perseverance).

When we feel the pain of what has long been missing, that discomfort may be a recognition of our role in the severance and a longing for the endowments of the shadow side of our culture.

There probably never will be a cultural center without margins. Even some margins have margins, as in the homeless encampment on the toxic waste dump. But it is in our own best interests to help make our cultural margins as minimal and as pain-free as possible so that when, with time, we each discover that we, too, have become marginalized, we will not be so far outcast as otherwise we might.

The best way to ease our own potential isolation and marginalization is to begin now to share our humble presence with our extended human family. Those who choose to go to the margins, and to return to the middle, and go back again to the margins, create a subtle motion,

much like that of an art gum eraser sliding across a line that wasn't supposed to have been drawn on a paper. We can use our own willingness to approach the margins to help erase the dividing lines, opening the outside and the center to each other a little more each time the line is crossed.

However much we might wish to reach out, a habit of self-protectiveness buried within may still hold us back. "Keep the doors locked and we'll be secure," says the ego. Our heart responds, "But I'm not happy like that."

—Ram Dass and Paul Gorman, *How Can I Help?*

8

DO YOU DARE?

*H*aving come this far in the book, you have read about the margins of our culture and about the people who inhabit them. Perhaps you acknowledge reasons why, if you dared, you might go to some of those places and interact with some of those people.

But do you dare to do so?

Does that voice in your mind say, "Keep the doors locked"? Or is your heart telling you, "But I'm not happy like that"?

Knowing why you might approach the margins is one thing; actually doing it is another. How does one prepare for the journey toward such an unknown region? How might you overcome your resistances?

It helps if you have discovered your own fears and begun to understand them. And it helps if you develop some "margin smarts": ways of being on the streets and in the margins that may ensure your welcome and your safety. In this chapter you'll learn that you can also go to the

people of the margins with your mind and heart, even if you don't dare to go in person. But first I invite you to look at two tasks that can prepare you to go into the margins.

You Can Dare if You Clarify Your Fears

Digging deeper beneath the question, "Do I dare to go into the margins?" you will find there is another, more poignant question: "If so, how do I keep from being afraid?"

We'd all like not to fear, but fear is hardwired into us. Fear prolongs our survival. The prepare-to-run-or-to-fight command triggered by a squirt of adrenaline into the bloodstream is a chemistry we cannot change, and wouldn't want to even if we could. Fear is essential to us and, at least for me, it never goes away. In an emergency room, or at the bedside of a man struggling to die, or on the rancid streets where homeless people hide, I may look unruffled, but almost always I feel fear. Sometimes, under my breath, I even resort to the perky little melody from *The King and I*: "Whenever I feel afraid / I hold my head erect / and whistle a happy tune / so no one will suspect / I'm afraid," and it takes days for the annoying song to go away again.

But if I try to selectively numb my fear, my vulnerability, and all the difficult feelings, I end up also numbing my joy and happiness. For, in their complexity, all emotions are attached to each other.

Yet, if I don't want to be afraid and I can't *not* be afraid, what then?

For myself, I've learned to ask slightly different questions: first, "What kind of fear is it that I am feeling now?" and then, "Is this kind of fear useful to me?"

It is helpful to realize that there are different "flavors" of fear. It is not useful to be swirled around by a vortex of generalized fear. What, specifically, do I fear? Is what I'm feeling fear of pain? Is it fear of scarcity? Is it fear of loss? Is it fear of fear? Can I be more specific? Am I afraid that the woman in that bed will die in the next five minutes? Am I afraid that I won't know what to do when she dies? Am I afraid that because I'm here, I'll somehow be held accountable for her dying? Am I afraid that if I see death, death might see me and choose me? If I can whittle my fear down to its smallest component, it becomes much more manageable than an amorphous blob of terror.

Fear of the Unknown

A few primary, unwhittled fears rise in me, especially when I approach society's margins: Fear of What-I've-Not-Yet-Experienced-but-if-I-Do-It-Might-Be-Awful is at the top of my list. Its shorter name is Fear of the Unknown. It's the stuff that comprises monsters hiding in the closet. It is a foreboding of tight-lipped disapproval from others. It is dread of going to a party filled with strangers. It is a certainty that something unpredictable is going to go wrong. Fear of the unknown is my recurring nightmare of walking out onto a stage to act a part for which I have never learned the script. Fear of the unknown reinforces what-ifs, assures me that I'll get lost, warns me not to try something new because I don't know how it will turn out. Fear of the unknown is my fear of death. Though I've watched dozens of people die, not one of them has ever returned to tell me exactly what the transition was like and

what's on the other side, and so death is another unknown for me to fear.

But it is useful to me to know that it's not monsters or public presentations or even death in general that I really fear; more specifically I fear what comes immediately *after* those things—being eaten alive by the monster, being embarrassed by a booing audience, being vaporized into nothingness by death. But since I haven't even met up with the monster yet, nor stepped in front of the audience, nor been given a short prognosis, my fear is getting way ahead of me, and I'm exhausting myself unnecessarily by fearing the unknown.

<div align="center">❧</div>

The Fearsome Dark Animal

For years I had a repetitive dream about a dark animal that chased me. I would wake up with heart pounding and adrenaline surging. When I told a friend about my dream, she suggested that the next time it occurred, if I could manage to stay asleep, I should turn around in the dream and face the creature.

I went home questioning the friend's own mental state, but a few nights later I was aware that I was having that same dream again. Still asleep, I turned around, wondering whether, if you get killed in a dream, you are still alive to wake up afterward.

I faced the dark animal.

It turned out to be a chocolate-colored Labrador retriever that desperately wanted to take me to a pretty clearing in the woods; she wanted me sit beside her and stroke her head. The dream may have been a foreshadowing of the massage therapy

practice that would later find me, a dream created by my unconscious trying to prepare me for the huge changes in my life that practice would lead to.

Making the unknown known is done by naming the fear, facing it, and following it to encounter what has been avoided.

༄

Fear of Physical Harm

My second primary fear in the margins is Fear of Physical Harm. The possibility of being attacked seems to loom large in imagining street work or work in a psychiatric hospital. Further on in this chapter you'll read some basic rules of street smarts, and how attitude, expectations, and behavior provide the best security on the streets. Similarly, hospitals and nursing homes have well-defined protocols for behavior and safety. The fact is that, unless several of those street rules or institutional protocols are ignored, you are not likely to be in danger in either place. In the months I spent working in a psychiatric hospital and on the psychiatric unit in a medical hospital, I was never aware of being in danger of physical harm. In my five years of working in the very "worst" places in San Francisco, I was in physical danger three times (that I know of). Let me tell you those stories.

༄

Three "Close Calls"?

Once, on Jones Street, just down the hill from Golden Gate Avenue, a homeless woman was sitting on the milk crate that

I sometimes carried as a massage chair. My Care Through Touch Institute partner that day was Dale, and he kept watch over the woman and me and the street, so I could fully concentrate on my work. We were about ten minutes into the massage; my eyes were closed, and I was in that timeless, placeless, intuitive space to which massage work can transport a therapist. Dimly I heard the sounds of a fight breaking out somewhere. I knew Dale would tell me if we needed to move, so I kept on with the massage. The fight sounds came closer, then receded, then blended into the general background noises of the city. I finished the massage, hugged the woman, and walked on down the street with Dale.

"Thanks, Dale, for keeping us safe during that massage," I said.

"I didn't do anything," he said. "The fight never came over to our side of the street." He was quiet for a moment as we walked, until we had to wait for a stoplight. "What you didn't know back there," he continued, "was that three street people were hanging around us, prepared to protect you and me and the woman you were working on if they were needed."

I turned around to find and thank those unnoticed guardians, but they, like the sounds and the incident itself, had already disappeared into the milieu of street life.

In a second incident, I was scheduled to offer seated massages in the lobby of a Tenderloin SRO hotel. I was early and waiting for Don, my Care Through Touch Institute partner for the day. I stood in front of the building, watching to my left for Don to come from the direction of Taylor Street. I heard an angry shout nearby and turned to my right at the same time that a hand gripped my left shoulder and pulled me back into the hotel entryway. "I think you'd rather

be back here," a gravelly voice said into my left ear, just as two entangled bodies crashed to the sidewalk right where I'd been standing a second earlier.

The two men struggled fiercely; the one on top yelled, "Don't fight me, man! Don't fight me!" and a minute later he had bound the other man's wrists with a thin strap of plastic. It was a drug bust, and the plainclothes cop—the guy on top—was sweating and out of breath.

I turned around and thanked the homeless man who, having more street smarts than I, had gotten me out of harm's way. He looked into my eyes, nodded once, and shuffled on.

The third incident happened early in my work on the streets, and there was no way I could have been prepared for it. I was walking toward the corner of Ellis and Hyde, intending to cross the street, when from a hidden place around the corner, a shard of glass flew across my path and shattered on the curb. I pulled back a few yards, crossed the street in the middle of the block, and from the other side was able to watch a man near the corner holding a paper grocery bag, apparently filled with many more shards of glass. He muttered to himself, staggered around a little, shouted an invective, and pitched another shard of glass, not at anything or anyone in particular but perhaps at life in general. Several people were watching with me, and one of them said she'd gone into the liquor store and asked them to call the cops to come collect this guy until he settled down.

❧

Never, in five years of street work, did I experience violence, anger, or even the threat of malice or intentional harm directed at me. What I learned in all three of these

incidents was the potential for random violence. But being in the wrong place at the wrong time can happen anywhere, anywhen, not just in the margins. If we sequester ourselves in our own homes, there is still no guarantee that we won't be injured by a fire or a fall, an errant paring knife or a neighbor who's suddenly gone berserk. Fear of random violence remains a realistic concern for me, and it's one of the ordinary risks of living. Street smarts diminish the risks considerably, as does the kindness of strangers. Wisdom and kindness are of value everywhere. But there are no guarantees of total safety anywhere, least of all in the margins.

Do you dare to go there nevertheless? Margaret Wheatley writes:

> We can't restore sanity to the world, but we can still remain sane and available. We can still aspire to be of service wherever need summons us. We can still focus our energy on working for good people and good causes. It is never too late to be brave.

Can you consider your own fears and still "be brave"?

Fear of Contagion

I said I have two main fears, but I must admit I have yet another one. This fear shows up as a vague unease, and it took me a long time to recognize it for what it was. Now I know that it is Fear That Death or Mental Illness or Even Poverty Might Somehow Be Contagious. I am afraid that I might catch the "disease" of marginalization. If I hang around the margins too much (or at all), I myself might become crazy, or homeless, or dead.

Well, in spite of the fact that I've often said "She drives me crazy" and "This work will be the death of me," neither death nor mental illness is physically infectious, though they can feel emotionally infectious. For all of us, death is the only certainty, and to be around a lot of dying people confirms death beyond a doubt, but it does not make death *happen*. Craziness is a matter of degree and a matter of circumstances, so each of us is at various times a little crazy and sometimes more than a little, but mental illness is not something like the flu that we catch through contact.

Yet marginalization, and even homelessness, can happen to absolutely anyone, far more easily than we'd like to imagine. It has nothing to do with contagion and everything to do with social safety nets. The fall from the middle to the margins happens when our safety nets are weak or torn and can't hold. Listen to the stories of two homeless men who remembered well the safety nets that couldn't support them in their fall to the streets.

❧

Slow-Motion Fall

It's Tuesday morning, and I'm working in one of San Francisco's ubiquitous daytime drop-in centers for homeless people. Decades ago, the place was a storefront facing Jones Street. Now the hazy plate-glass windows have a golden patina of nicotine grime on the inside, and a film of gray auto exhaust is permanently etched into the outside surfaces. The window display areas that once showed products or produce for sale to potential customers now offer generations of dead flies along the edges, yellowed newspapers strewn

about, and stacks of magazines with rumpled covers like small unmade beds. The grit and residue in this place should bother me, but they don't, because on this particular day I am far more disgusted by the sugar.

On a table at the back of this gloomy room are open boxes of two-day-old glazed donuts, sweating and soggy with the city's humidity; an urn of terrible coffee flanked by stacks of petroleum-based polystyrene cups; shakers of powdered coffee-whitener made from sugar and heart-clogging trans fats; and a box of packets of sugar. Breakfast for the people of the streets: empty calories for worthless lives. Surely we could do better than this! With all the addictions in this room, do we have to push sugar and toxins on them as well?

When William walks in, I am giving a seated massage, but I shouldn't be. I am in a cranky mood, disgusted by the stale sugary shit on offer, and I know very well that "cranky" can be transmitted straight through my hands to the body of the person I am touching. Just seeing William reminds me of my responsibility; I take deep breath, set aside my judgments, finish the massage in peace, and then go to sit with William.

William is a few inches over six feet tall, in his early fifties, with graying brown hair still thick and wavy. His rich brown eyes survey wherever he is, and they don't miss a thing. His posture shows off his broad shoulders; he always wears a sport coat and collared shirt, and often a tie. He seldom says much, but conversations with him are wonderful because he has a knack for asking questions that seek personal answers that he actually wants to hear. He responds with his eyes and his receptive face. William is a strong advocate for homeless people; he is compassionate, and articulate when he does speak. He has a law degree and once was a practicing

attorney; he is now a homeless man, a street person, standing in soup kitchen queues for his meals, waiting in line for public toilets, sleeping in homeless shelters, eating crappy, sweaty donuts at drop-in shelters.

Mostly I don't ask street people about Before. Some offer the information, often in the afterglow of a chair massage. Those who talk about Before want me to understand that they once were somebody, or at least that their nobody status was someone else's fault. But most street people don't want to discuss any time on either side of today, and usually I don't ask questions.

However, a few months earlier, I asked William about the sport coat he always wears, and he answered, "Force of habit." I raised an eyebrow at that, and he heard the implied question. That's when he told me he'd been an attorney, disbarred six years before. A dozen more questions appeared on my face like a sudden rash that I didn't dare scratch. Some of the itchy questions he answered; most he didn't.

What became clear is that during the progress of his gradual descent, despite his education and his connections and his finances, William's social safety net was finally too weak to hold him. In one of the longest disclosures I ever heard him make, he said, "It was like I was standing on a rooftop and tripped over the edge. After that, everything was slow motion: like being caught by the branch of a tree. That held for a while, then cracked under my weight." With his long-fingered hands he sketched the fall in the space above our table. "Like in a bad dream . . . I fell again, and was saved by a lower branch. That finally gave up, and I crashed to the ground." His palm landed flat on the surface of the drop-in shelter's table. In silence, we both stared at the

gesture. His motionless hand was far more eloquent than a longer story would have been.

Now, at the far end of our table, a man named George begins to snore, his head heavy, his face contorted on his arms folded in front of him on the table. His open mouth drools a little on his sleeves. From eight feet away we can smell the alcohol on his breath. William gets up, shakes George gently by the shoulder, and says, "Hey, buddy, gotta sit up if you're gonna sleep here." Sleeping on the tables isn't allowed in this drop-in center. If you can sleep sitting up and not fall out of your chair, that is allowed. Most street people have perfected this knack, but being drunk compromises almost any skill. It is raining outside, and William doesn't want his friend to get kicked back out into the weather.

George's journey, too, was a long slow fall to the streets. Unlike William, he still talks a lot and almost always asks for a massage when he sees me. The first time I massaged his hands he told me that he was a structural engineer; his specialty was the design of airport control towers. I had no reason to disbelieve him—or to believe him, for that matter, because he was pretty drunk that day, too. But there was a quality of desperation behind his eyes, a plea to be taken seriously, that made me think he wasn't bullshitting me. He said he'd last worked in Omaha but had been in San Francisco "for a while."

A few weeks later I was massaging George's shoulders, and he picked up the thread of his story almost as if there had been no intervening pause. He'd been injured in an auto accident in Nebraska. "Your left side?" I asked; my hands had felt how unyielding his musculature was on that side. He nodded. He had been driving, and was sideswiped on an icy road; one of his children, a son, was killed in the collision.

The grief and the guilt, combined with an increase in the alcohol that numbed them, gradually grew into a huge marital wedge, and he and his wife divorced a few years later. He couldn't focus on his work, and he lost his job. He wore out his welcome with friends and their living room sofas. He couldn't get a grip on his drinking. One branch after another gave way, and life finally dropped him into the Tenderloin.

William props George upright in his chair; he folds George's good right arm across his chest and tucks it under the left arm, then pulls the left hand into the crook of George's right armpit in the classic sleeping-upright position. George's chin drops immediately to his chest, and he is asleep again in the approved manner, balanced upright in the chair.

By now it is almost ten a.m., time for William to show up at the thrift store where he does odd jobs and writes the monthly fundraising newsletter in exchange for an occasional sport coat in his size and some collared shirts.

There are two dozen other street people around the tables of the drop-in center today, watching TV, playing cards, and eating donuts. Which of them were once successful salespeople, performers, doctors, homemakers, artists, entrepreneurs? I know that one man, for a year, was a pro football player; and one woman has shown me recognizable photos of herself as a professional dancer.

Life at the margins may be, for anyone, only one illness away or one accident or divorce away, one addiction, or a single misstep from "the edge of the roof" away. Destitution seems to have little to do with genetics or family status; it has mostly to do with fragile social connections that give way under the weight of whatever our particular fall may be. It has to do with those "branches" that can't support us any longer.

All of us, all the time, are so very close to that line that separates us from the margins. Our environment is increasingly unable to support our health; our mortgages and investments are evaporating; our social support programs are underfunded and closing their doors; our families are fractured and dispersed; all of us are aging and dying. And we don't want to see these factors any more than we want to see William the lawyer and George the engineer, who have fallen into the margins just one step ahead of us, who may already have drunk all the terrible coffee and finished off the crappy sugary glazed donuts just before we arrive.

❧

There is one advantage to thinking about the things I fear as contagious: it makes me more willing to try out the idea of inoculation. A learning edge of service work is wondering how it might feel to be in the presence of what one fears, "trying on" the fear, practicing, rehearsing just in case. This "trying on" is like a vaccination or like homeopathy: a small dose of what I fear, to prevent that same thing from seeming so big and so overwhelming that, when it does appear in my life, it paralyzes and endangers me. Inoculation by imagination seems to me like just what the doctor might order to help me risk going into the margins.

Having been to the margins, having seen myself in the faces of the people I meet there and having seen my possible future in their squalid present, is a huge impetus to my desire to open trails between the margins and the center. I want the pathways to and from the margins to be well used by the time I get there. It will be hard enough to be marginalized by society's opinions of my aging and my

health and my financial status without also being isolated from any interactions with the center. So now, while I still can, I add my footprints to the paths that cross the line.

YOU CAN DARE IF YOU DEVELOP STREET SMARTS

Do you dare to go into the margins? If so, it's essential that you learn street smarts, that you learn how a person should behave at the far edge of the margins.

"On the streets" seems to be the scariest venue in the margins. People ask me, "But how do you keep yourself safe out there?" They almost never ask that question about my similar ventures into nursing homes or hospitals or private homes.

It doesn't come with any guarantees, but the short course in "margin smarts" I'm now going to offer you has kept me safe all these years, so you may draw your own conclusions. This is the curriculum: Pay attention, monitor your attitude, and use your fear wisely.

Pay Attention

When I walk on the streets, or in a mall parking lot, or in any unfamiliar place, I remind myself to pay attention. How many people are nearby? What are they wearing? Are they particularly aware of me? What are the smells and the sounds around me? What (or who) do I think is just around that next corner, or under that pile of cardboard beside the dumpster? I look up, into second- or third-story windows. What's going on all around me? Who is behind me? This is not paranoia; this is attention, alertness.

Years after I left San Francisco a Seattle massage therapist asked if I'd teach her how to give street massages. So I spent a day showing her the techniques and sharing some of my stories. Then a few weeks later, I took her to the huge shadowy parking area beneath Interstate 5 at Seattle's James Street exit to try out her skills. After I pulled in and shut off the engine of my car, I invited Robin to look around and tell me how many homeless people she saw. She noticed two leaning against a pillar supporting the overpass, one leaning against the cyclone fence at the far side, and four others walking or standing nearby. I noticed five additional people—two lying together in a blanket at the base of a dumpster, one sitting on the opposite side of a pillar so just his knee was visible, and another two huddled between parked cars. When we got out of our car to begin our massage work, it was important that we knew where everyone else was so that we could remain aware and alert, and so that we could include everyone in the kind of compassionate energy we hoped to bring to the streets that day.

Monitor Your Attitude

When I am in the margins, what do I intuit? What am I feeling in my body? Whatever I am feeling and reacting to in my body is a combination of expectations and attitudes, both mine and those of others around me. Expectation and attitude determine most of what anyone will encounter on the streets.

Attitude can be conveyed by body language and clothing; sometimes it can be faked by posturing and sham. But genuine attitudes, the real expectations of the streets,

are an invisible energy that exudes into the atmosphere like pheromones, swirling and mixing with all the other nearby attitudes to create the complex perfume of presence on the streets. One sniff and an experienced street person knows what's up and who's in charge. And possibly where the cash for the next meal is coming from.

Yes, there are some people on the streets who are hunting for easy prey. I won't pretend that's not true. So when you choose to enter that world, your first task is to "cop an attitude"—make sure you look as if you won't be worth the time or effort—and those few who are on the prowl will move on to other, easier quarry.

Don't carry a purse (keep everything in pants or skirt pockets), don't flash money, and don't look helpless or scared, no matter how you're feeling inside.

Walk purposefully and mindfully—keep moving, keep your head up, move with authority, and look as confident and full-bodied as possible. Everything about you should say, *I'm on my way. I know where I'm going.*

It helps a lot if this is true. Prepare ahead of time—this is not the ideal time or place to be uncertain or lost. Even if you become lost, keep moving. If you have to get help with directions, choose a well-lit shop or agency office, go in as if that is your destination, and ask a clerk for the information you need.

The easiest safety measure of all is to have another person along with you—the hunters don't want to work that hard. But be sure that both of you remain alert. Don't distract each other from maintaining your external attitudes.

You also need to monitor your internal attitudes. If your intention is to interact with people, what you need is a

state of nonjudgmental calm. This is your passport to the margins. It will serve you well in many venues, from the roughest areas of a large city to a rural high school parking lot.

Though it was unspoken, and remains mostly unconscious, many of us were taught what I call the Rule—the social imperative saying that we should not have to see or deal with marginalized people, those "others," whether they are homeless or ill or even that odd transitional form of humanity called a teen. The Rule says that we are above the "others" in some unspecified way, and shouldn't have to see or interact with them.

If you are going to go to the margins, leave behind the Rule, with its negative judgments, along with all the rest of your assumptions. Those assumptions become a strong, irritating aroma on the streets (or at that high school parking lot), and can be detected a block away.

Please notice that this street-smarts advice is given from a different perspective than the typical staying-safe guidebook (*Tough Target* by J. J. Bittenbinder is a good one, by the way). If you go into the margins intending to offer intangible gifts, or for any other compassionate reason, the point is to interact, not to avoid interaction. There is a difference between your choosing to approach a marginalized person, and being approached by someone on the streets. If you are approached and you sense aggression, trust your instincts—say, "No!" and walk away quickly. If there was no harm intended, you may have lost an opportunity, but you will be safe.

Once when I was walking in the Tenderloin with Mary Ann Finch, three men walking toward us stopped and

stood in our way. "Well, look what we got us here," one of them said, eyeing all five-foot-nothing of Mary Ann's 110 pounds.

Mary Ann took two steps toward him, looked straight up into his eyes, and said with a calm, level voice, "Don't. Just *don't*."

The men parted silently, and Mary Ann walked forward as I followed in her wake, holding my breath and trying to look strong.

Use Your Fear Wisely

More advice: Use your fear wisely, to keep yourself alert, not paralyzed. Always stay public, out where other people are; do not get into a car or go into an alleyway with someone. And if there is an act of aggression, make as much noise as you can: yell, "FIRE!" loudly, over and over again, as you run away. (People pay attention to "FIRE!" because it might have implications for their own safety. If you yell, "HELP!" they may feel their own safety is compromised by responding to you.) The person with bad intentions will probably decide to take his efforts somewhere less noisy.

If you dare, and choose to go into the margins, you may trust that there is also an amazing amount of kindness on the streets and elsewhere every single day. I recommend that you look for it, and amplify it by offering kindness when you can. Seeing kindness will help balance out your fear. And an attitude of kindness, even just a no-strings-attached smile, will incrementally shift the balance of good available to you and to everyone else on the streets.

And If You Still Don't Dare . . .

If you are moved by stories of marginalized people, if you wish you *could* dare to cross that line and even sit at the feet of these profound teachers, but you just can't bring yourself to do it . . . all is not lost. There are yet other ways to develop marginal eyes and be with the people of the margins. And there are other ways to participate in the erasing of the boundaries between the middle and the margins. You might . . .

Practice Composting the News

Rather than entering the margins yourself, let journalists and others go to the war zones, to the streets, to disaster sites, to all the margins around the world, while you make it a practice to contemplate what is brought to the doorstep of your mind through television, radio, online news, or print media. Contemplation is a way of considering the news, of turning your attention to whatever appears, and of holding that for a moment as a sacred teaching, no matter how painful or hopeless or inane it might seem. But then what do you do with it once you've held it?

My friends who compost their garbage have unintentionally shown me this way to respond: I try to notice every detail of whatever has presented itself to me. I try to take it all in without judging any of it as good or bad or beautiful or ugly. In my mind I assemble all of what I've noticed and then I imagine wrapping it up and placing it into the ground below me to be assimilated into the earth; I offer it

all to Mother Earth, who knows intimately about composting and change.

Since mostly I am not wise enough to know the difference between what can be changed and what can't, I trust the earth to sort through everything, to know what should be encouraged to grow and what should wither and rot to become something else altogether. I don't have to do anything except agree to gather what I see and spiritually pass it on to her, commending everything to her care.

I trust that the Spirit within Mother Earth can "compost" things like anger and fear and helplessness as easily as she composts orange rinds and grass clippings; I trust that she knows how to make compassion and vulnerability and love flourish in the recycled muck along with asters and ferns and fir trees. Furthermore, this same Spirit/Earth wisdom knows where the flourishing needs to happen —on a street corner, in the mind of a senator, or in my own heart. As I witness the suffering in our world, I know that spiritual composting changes me: I become more resilient, less afraid, more generous. And I believe that spiritual composting changes the world: anger and fear and helplessness are drawn away from the social field to make way for compassion and vulnerability in their place.

Given the great quantities of news available through the information superhighway, I recommend doing this meditation only in small bites/bytes so that you do not get overwhelmed. Otherwise, rather than allow yourself to be drowned in a tsunami of negative news that you can't get rid of fast enough, it might become less risky to just go the margins yourself.

Cynthia Trenshaw

Practice *Tonglen*

There is a Tibetan Buddhist practice of spiritual composting called *tonglen*. The word means "giving and taking." The variation of *tonglen* that I use is basically simple breathing. It begins with being aware of what is before me, particularly whatever is dark, uncomfortable, painful, helpless, marginalized, or socially invisible. I focus, then, on my willingness to be made useful and my prayer to be kept safe as I "breathe in" these sinister things. For the brief time between the in-breath and the out-breath, I imagine that whatever is negative and dark and hidden will be transformed within me, and then I exhale whatever is positive and light, for the benefit of all beings. Before the next in-breath I thank the Spirit that is able to accomplish the transformation from negative to positive so effortlessly. And that's the whole sequence, in the space of a single breath: notice, intend, breathe in darkness; intend, breathe out light, be grateful. Then repeat for however many breaths feel appropriate.

Pema Chödrön, a Buddhist nun with a wide following, teaches *tonglen* in this way on the Shambhala.org website:

> If you are out walking and you see someone in pain—right on the spot you can begin to breathe in their pain and send some out some relief. Or, more likely, you might see someone in pain and look away because it brings up your fear or anger; it brings up your resistance and confusion.
>
> So on the spot you can do tonglen for all the people who are just like you, for everyone who wishes to be compassionate but instead is afraid, for everyone who wishes to be brave but instead is a coward.

Pema continues (in *When Things Fall Apart*):

> Rather than beating ourselves up, we can use our personal stuckness as a stepping stone to understanding what people are up against all over the world. Breathe in for all of us and breathe out for all of us.

His Holiness the Dalai Lama is reported to practice *tonglen* every day; he has said of this technique, "Whether this meditation really helps others or not, it gives me peace of mind. Then I can be more effective, and the benefit is immense."

So it seems that even the gift of *tonglen* is reciprocal! This is the primary way that I handle the depressing things I see on the streets, in the news, or hidden away in private homes. And this is how I handle the distressing things in my own heart: when I am afraid, I try to practice *tonglen* for all others who are feeling afraid at this same moment; when I am in pain, I try to practice *tonglen* for all others who are in pain; when I am contemplating death, I do this breath practice for everyone who is dying at this moment. Sometimes I don't even set an intention with each breath; I simply ask at the beginning of the day, or at the start of a difficult part of a day, that my breathing be used in this transformative way. Then I just breathe through the day, trusting that my having asked, and being willing to participate, will be enough. And I offer a single heartfelt sigh of gratitude at the end of the day for all that has been transformed by the simple act of *tonglen* breathing.

Practice *Kything*

Another practice of personal spiritual connection is called *kything*. Madeleine L'Engle brought this word into popular usage in her book, *A Wind in the Door*, employing a word that she reportedly found in her Scottish grandfather's dictionary. Similar to telepathy, kything is a way of being present spirit-to-spirit, and communicating within that presence. A more complete description of the practice of kything can be found in *Kything: the Art of Spiritual Presence* by Louis M. Savary and Patricia H. Berne. Here I'll offer my simplified version:

Imagine that you are on your way to work, driving on a city freeway. Out of the corner of your eye you notice a homeless woman and her belongings tucked up into the narrow space where a sloping ridge of land meets the underside of an exit ramp. Ordinarily that image wouldn't even register in your mind, but today it does for some reason, and it stays with you, returning to your consciousness throughout your morning. So during your lunch break you decide to practice kything with that particular woman, to let her know that she is not alone, that you have noticed her and care about her.

To start, quiet your mind and be present to your own spirit, knowing that this is a spiritual practice you are about to undertake. Then focus on the woman you saw earlier in the day; remember her in as much detail and with as much intensity as you can until you feel your spirit is present to her spirit. Now envision yourself and the woman together, and choose to make that encounter a reality. This choosing is the step that transcends imagination and puts into motion

what is needed to realize your intention to be with the woman. From this point on, it is up to you to offer your intangible gifts, to receive her intangible gifts, to carry her story, and, when you are ready, to thank her and return to your ordinary day.

Kything can be done anywhere, anytime, with anyone, and, for that matter, with anything. The most important aspect to remember, however, is that the encounter must be unconditional, with no intention or effort on your part to control, change, or interfere with the one with whom you kythe. Just be present, and that will make all the difference.

PART THREE:

Seven Teachers

Once in a while you will stumble upon the truth
but most of us manage to pick ourselves up and
hurry along as if nothing had happened.

—Winston Churchill

9

AN INVITATION

At the beginning of this book you heard the voice of Gloria, whose understanding of reciprocity underlies everything I learned in the margins. This woman of the streets knew that at the same time she received from me, she was also giving to me.

You've heard the stories I carried from the margins into the pages of these chapters, and the six lessons that were gifted to me from my teachers there: initiation into the journey, the meaning of touch, barriers to giving, the importance of intention, what it means to have enough, what it means to be enough.

I have asked two challenging questions: Why go there? Do you dare to go there? And I've tried to answer both questions from my personal experiences at the edges of our culture.

You've gotten this far in the book, and I applaud your courage for staying with it—these are not easy topics.

Now it is my pleasure to invite you into a special

collection of verbal portraits. Here you will meet seven beloved teachers whom I knew during my years of spiritual formation in the margins. Each of these teachers is hidden away in a different region of the margins of our culture, and each requires you to employ a different physical sense within your imagination.

I suggest that you approach these people as if you were able to be with them physically, so you can practice applying what you've learned in the earlier chapters of this book. Experience how it feels to offer your intangible gifts to each of these people. See what gifts they have to offer you in return. Receive their stories and carry those stories back into your daily life. Perhaps then practice *tonglen* or kything with them. As you are present in the margins in these ways, see how your appreciation expands.

To help you with this process, there are a few questions for you to consider at the end of each portrait. You may want to share these questions, and your responses to them, with a friend, or classmates, or a church discussion group, or a book club.

Here, now, are the seven special teachers: Eleanor, who will provoke your listening skills; Betty, who cannot be touched except by your eyes; Rayshawn, who is willing to taste brotherhood; Margaret, who can experience phantom touch; and Noreen Frances and Vera, who may offend your sense of smell. And then, after all these thousands of words, there is Mack who demands nothing more—and nothing less—than silent presence.

Your encounter with each of them may or may not be pleasant, but it *will* be instructive.

It will be a gift.

JABBERWOCKY

'*T*was brillig, and the slithy toves did gyre
and gimble in the wabe . . .

*I glanced up into the restroom mirror and saw the silly
smile on my face. To my own image I whispered the next part
of Lewis Carroll's nonsense poem:* ". . . all mimsy were
the borogoves, / and the mome raths outgrabe."

*I was trying to keep a straight face, but it was hopeless.
Wonderland's grinning Cheshire Cat stared right back at me.
Fluorescent light glinted off the porcelain fixtures; it sparkled
on the nursing home's antiseptic-white ceramic tiles. I was
tempted, just for the helluvit, to tug the pull-this-cord-for-
help string on the wall: that room needed livening up, and it
definitely needed more color! Having just been with Eleanor,
I was in a wonderfully silly mood.*

*When I first met her, Eleanor was sitting in her wheel-
chair across from the activities bulletin board. Autumn leaves
and construction paper pumpkins were scattered around
announcements of bingo (2:30 M, W, F), exercise class
(9:30 T, Th), rhythm band (4:00 W), and the week's
dining room menu. I was headed toward another hall, tossing
just a smile and a nod to Eleanor on my way.*

*But before I got past her, she had grabbed my skirt and
caught my attention. My bright-colored skirt had a playful
chevron of fringe on the front, and Eleanor was fascinated by*

the fringe. She gently fingered each strand as if it were fragile and wonderful beyond words. She wheeled her chair with one hand and accompanied me to the end of the hall, fondling the fringe all the way.

Later that day I noticed Eleanor again. She was holding a soft plush toy dog, and wanted to tell me all about the "baby" in her arms. "Baby here holding, gribolz," she said. "Ears popper up, and eyes. Biffitt."

"Ah," I said, in a brilliant moment of translation, "you said your baby's eyes and ears are beautiful."

Eleanor looked at me as if I were crazy.

"Rain-sun fretz, and . . . crumber," she emphasized for someone to whom she had to explain things in such simple terms.

I was employed by this nursing home as a part-time massage therapist. I mentioned that to Eleanor, and to demonstrate, I began to massage one of her hands. Although hand massage usually soothes and relaxes a patient, Eleanor fidgeted and twisted in her chair and couldn't stay focused. After just a minute she pulled her hand back. She was decidedly not interested.

The fact is that I had failed to ask her permission to touch her. I'd fallen into a common, ugly assumption: if Eleanor couldn't talk straight, she couldn't think straight. I could exercise my "prerogative" of deciding for her, and I had decided that she should want a hand massage.

She did not.

On Friday, Eleanor parked her wheelchair under the same bulletin board where we'd first met. She was scanning every detail of the materials pinned there, muttering to herself. "It's just plurbik, and here kitter stippel." She

considered the items in the left-hand corner. "I like the pogs. Bumping stongs on Friday jing."

I pulled up a chair next to her and listened to her for a while. She looked from me to the notices and back to me, saying excitedly, "Dollivest going from here and longer to ronnifer." Straining to see what she might be referring to, I began to read some of the notices to her, to see if anything caught her interest. Eleanor stared at me silently, with increasing impatience. She didn't look back at the bulletin board, just stared at me. I tried again, reading a tacked-up newspaper article about the nursing home, hoping to connect on some level with her earlier enthusiasm. But Eleanor folded her soft doggy baby into her armpit and slowly wheeled away from me.

I was a failure, rejected by a patient I was supposed to be serving. Worse, I was obviously boring to a woman who had only a nominally functioning brain! My ego was seriously bruised.

A week later my ego had recovered, and Eleanor's doctor had signed the approval form for massage therapy for her. I knelt in front of her, explained again about massage, and asked if that sounded good to her. She looked into my eyes and did not resist. Tentatively I reached up to stroke her left shoulder and upper arm.

"I have some bliggerts there," she said. And finally my own ever-so-slow brain cells began to fire and light up in a new equation: listening plus patience minus expectations equals communication.

"You have some bliggerts there?" I replied. "Well, let's see if this helps." And I stood to begin an abbreviated massage of her shoulders and arms and upper back.

"Ginger," she said. "Long time ago Jerry beaching. I saw. Frutter, I think."

"Frutter," I said. "I think so too." Gently I worked her biceps muscle, then cradled her left elbow and stretched her upper arm a bit. "Tell me about Jerry."

Eleanor was delighted. "Jerry, Jerry, Jerry," she said. "Brother, Father went with me. Pizza too, and letterons."

"Pizza and letterons, both at the same time?" I exclaimed.

"Uh-huh. Norming." She sighed, remembering. "I had a dress and shoes. Just like my dobbet."

"Just like your dobbet," I affirmed.

"It was a wall of weeks. Scrazzled. Under the papers, berking. I wrote sand and logs and pretty."

"Logs and pretty?" I asked, resisting the urge to decipher what I thought she meant, just letting her own flow of words carry us both.

"Uh-huh. We went in the car. Incattering and trees. And Baby," she said, looking fondly at the toy in her lap.

Her right forearm was relaxing in my hands now, and I was working toward the wrist. "Did Baby like the trees?" I ventured.

"Oh no, Baby was scarfelled." She smiled dotingly, amused at how scarfelled Baby could become. Then Eleanor yawned. We had been together for ten minutes now, a new record. "Done," said Eleanor, and yawned again. She hugged Baby to her chest. I kissed her gently on the cheek, and told her we'd do massage together again soon.

Somewhere in Eleanor's brain, the "we" of that promise rang literally. The next time I approached her, kneeling in front of her and reminding her of who I was, she took my hand and began massaging it. "Massagerwints," she said

proudly. *Tears sprang to my eyes, and I responded, "Massager-wints," as if acknowledging a champagne toast.*

A few days later, a brief rainfall had ended and sun was beginning to sparkle on the potted plants in the nursing home's courtyard. Eleanor was waiting in her wheelchair by the courtyard door, eager to talk about something that was "not ready yet."

"It's not ready yet," I said, launching us into our special way of conversing.

"Coming after criglens," she assured me, and we were off again, letting go to the making and receiving of the sounds of words. Eleanor took the lead, because she understood the meanings better than I did. In the cadence and the vibration of our human skill of speaking, we played with joy.

Over the coming months I continued to massage Eleanor's arms and hands. From time to time she reciprocated, stroking her thumbs on the tops of my hands and delighting in my skin. She was gentle and firm with me, holding on to her dignity and her wisdom as tightly as she hugged her Baby. Our exchanges stretched past fifteen minutes, and Eleanor-speak became the language of the world we shared.

I found my way into dialogue with Eleanor, and she found her way into my heart.

> *O frabjous day! Callooh! Callay!*
> *[She] chortled in [her] joy.*
> —Lewis Carroll, *Through the Looking-Glass*

~

Reflection Questions

1. At first Eleanor did not want to be touched. Why might that have been? How did she convey this?

2. How might you communicate with someone whose language you don't understand? With someone who doesn't understand your language?

3. Eleanor's language was partially English. What makes that a barrier to conversation with her?

4. What technique did the author eventually use to facilitate conversation? Could that technique be used or adapted with someone who is mute?

SHELTERED WOMAN

"One tough old broad," Betty usually calls herself, though she is only in her late thirties and so thin that nothing about her is "broad."

As for her being "tough," at the moment she is trembling in fear and pain.

Betty was discharged from the hospital about two hours ago. Her left arm is in a sling, her T-shirt is ripped, and her jeans are bloody and torn. Her face and arms are an abstract composition of emerging bruises. Large areas of her body are painfully abraded; her skin weeps lymph and her swollen eyes leak tears. She looks like something created by the special effects department for a second-rate horror movie. Except that this is the real thing. She cringes as I walk toward her, terrified of anyone coming near her raw skin.

I sit down on the floor of the homeless shelter, next to Betty's cot, and speak carefully, as one might speak to an injured bird who, if she tries to fly, will make the damage worse. My hands rest in my lap, in sight and unmoving, and I assure Betty that I will not touch her. For a long while no words pass between us as the sounds of shelter life rise and fall beyond the thin plywood walls that separate this huge open room from the rest of the former warehouse.

The women's dorm of the county homeless shelter can hold seventy or eighty cots, plus a staff desk and two folding

chairs. At full capacity there are about sixteen inches, on all sides, between one cot and another. Women with "sen-iority"—those who have been at the shelter, and obeyed the rules, for the most consecutive days—get beds along the walls. They are exposed to other people on only three sides. In a wall cot you can have your back to the wall, or even turn away from the woman snoring next to you. The four corners of the dorm are the most coveted spaces—there, two whole sides of a bed belong solely to the corner-dweller, and the be-longings crammed under her cot have some darkness to hide in.

Betty has no seniority, though she's lived in the shelter for two years. She sometimes leaves the shelter for several nights at a time, and she doesn't pay much attention to rules. So she seems always to be starting over, "on probation." Which means her assigned space is usually out in the center of the dorm. All of the beds are military surplus: old creaky wooden cots with sagging canvas, or newer aluminum ones with board-tight woven nylon. There is no way that Betty's damaged body can find comfort lying on her bed. So she sits. And I sit on the floor at her feet. And together we wait for whatever story might, or might not, be waiting to be told.

Betty plays with the edges of her assigned blanket, a quilt printed with ludicrous images of Barbie and pink stars. Blankets are one of the most valuable commodities for the people of the streets; the blankets in this shelter's women's dorm range from discarded moth-eaten wool to donated flowery ruffled bedspreads; most are the ubiquitous recycled-fiber gray blankets routinely doled out to homeless folks. Ordinarily Betty would not tolerate a Barbie blanket; she would barter with (or beat up) someone for a different one.

But this isn't an ordinary day for Betty. The fact that she

is even sitting on her cot at one p.m. is proof of that. All residents have to leave the shelter from ten a.m. to noon; then, after lunch, they may not use their cots again until two thirty unless they have written permission for bed rest. They have to be at their cot to answer roll call at seven o'clock nightly, or lose their space; if that happens, their belongings will be removed from the dorm and disposed of if not claimed within three days. Curfew is usually nine o'clock, ten on Friday and Saturday nights—be late and you lose your cot. Leave the premises after curfew, and you can't get back in till morning.

Finally, Betty's story begins to seep out. "I went out last night, and this happened."

I wait, silent, receptive.

"Well, yeah, I went off the property to meet with my friend Connie and smoke a joint." She shifts position, and winces with pain. "We met over in the vacant lot, by those brown warehouses."

I nod and listen, saying nothing.

"And then some bastard comes along and gets a strangle-hold on me, with a knife in his hand." She moves her right hand to the torn neckband of her shirt and lifts her chin. The knife had made two straight shallow cuts. "But he wasn't happy with just that. Maybe I didn't show enough fear." She snorts ironically, and tears begin to spill down her face. She hates being afraid. But not as much as she hates crying.

"He had my left arm behind me, and he yanked on it so hard he dislocated my shoulder." She raises her arm and sling to show me, and yelps with pain. Instinctively I move toward her, but quickly reconsider. She closes her eyes and bites her lip so her lip will hurt more than her shoulder.

"Then when I couldn't fight him anymore, the sonof-

a bitch grabbed two bricks and started beating me with them. Bricks, man. I've never ever been beaten like that before!"

I think, Jesus, woman, I've never ever been beaten, period.

Betty doesn't explain how she got to the hospital. Maybe her friend came back after the beating stopped. The hospital examined Betty and gave her the sling, some Tylenol for the pain, and a bus token for getting back to the shelter. She has no insurance and no money; they did the most they could do for her in a county emergency room filled with stabbings and gunshot wounds, overdoses and heart attacks and fevered children. They released Betty with blood still all over her body. Where the bricks scraped away her flesh, it is so painful that the slightest pressure of her T-shirt's fabric sends shock waves through her.

"Betty, I'd like to try to help you," I say.

She has enjoyed massage from me before, but she winces and whimpers, "No," as she imagines her flayed skin being stroked.

My hands remain still, in my lap. "I can do it without touching you," I say. "My hands will work with your body's energy above the skin."

"What good will that do?" she snorts skeptically.

"What harm will it do?" I reply.

She considers for a while, then nods. The pain is worse than her fear.

I sit with her on her cot, with enough distance between us so I won't accidentally brush her wounds. She closes her eyes as I begin with my hands to search through the energy fields around her body. My fingers hover over the open sores, and the knife marks at her throat. When she lets go to trust and

begins to feel the energy exchange between us, she starts to relax. Before long she sways from exhaustion. I help her to lie down on her less-damaged right side and slide a pillow under her head.

Two thirty rolls around. Other women begin entering the dorm. They see us and their conversations stop. They know what happened to Betty. They know it could have been one of them that was beaten. They watch Betty and me intently. Most of them don't like Betty, but they understand her pain.

The women move quietly to their own cots, still focused on us. Our space in the center of the women's dorm seems to grow denser, warmer, perhaps more filled with compassion than it was half an hour earlier.

Betty is asleep. Her forehead is still creased in pain, but her body is beginning its work of healing. Her psyche has a tougher job ahead. In one last fluid movement my hands trace the shape of her entire body, about four inches above her, from head to toe. For a little while, "one tough old broad" is safe, and sheltered, I hope, through whatever the coming night holds.

❧

Reflection Questions

1. In Betty's mugging, who do you think is at fault?

2. What do you think you would find most difficult about living in a homeless shelter? How could you adapt?

3. What else did you want to know about Betty? Would you have asked her? Why, or why not?

4. If you were one of the homeless onlookers, what would your thoughts have been?

EUCHARIST

The pager beside my pillow screams its triple alarm. My feet hit the tiled floor before my eyes open; the first surge of adrenaline hits my bloodstream before the pager speaks: "Chaplain, this is Emergency. We've got a gunshot down here, DOA. The family is on the way. Security is here. We need you stat." It is 1:45 a.m. Just twenty minutes earlier I crashed into a deep sleep, fully clothed, on the bed in the pastoral care on-call room. I knew better, knew that it doesn't pay to fall asleep on an overnight on-call shift: if I stayed awake, there wouldn't be any calls; if I fell asleep . . .

A splash of water on my face. Keys found, pen and notepad rounded up, and my name badge to give me access to whatever chaos waits in the emergency room. Out into the silent halls of the hospital annex, headed toward the main building. Wait for the elevator. Breathe. Allow the breath to become prayer: "Help me. Be present. Help them." That truncated prayer has become my litany, code words for everything that needs to be said between me and God in an emergency.

Ride the elevator down two floors, head through the shortcut, a musty-smelling tunnel lined with cables and wires and overhead pipes as big as ancient tree trunks. Out into the lab hallway. Punch in the code to the ER's staff entrance keypad. It has been eleven minutes from sound sleep to bright lights and organized chaos.

The ER secretary sits at the heart of it all, the epitome of multitasking, surrounded by phones, radios, monitors, and a wall of clipboards updated moment by moment. Like an air traffic controller at a busy airport, she coordinates the movements of patients, medical staff, technicians, ambulance crews, security, pastoral care. She slings her phone receiver onto her shoulder and briefs me: Dwayne, mid-twenties, shot in a bar fight on South Division Street. Dead. His friend, Rayshawn, with him in the bar, arrived with the ambulance; he is now in the chaplains' room near the triage area. He is "chemically impaired." The seasoned security officer who assessed Rayshawn advised the secretary that the chaplain should not to try to work with him; security will keep him out of the way in the chaplains' room for now, then remove him when the victim's family arrives. Ignoring the phone resting on her shoulder, the secretary picks up another phone and grabs a clipboard. She is moving on: impaired Rayshawn and deceased Dwayne are now "mine."

Moments later, Dwayne's mother, Jeannie, appears, breathless, alone, and terrified. I lead her to the admitting desk in the emergency waiting room and stand with her while she fills in the blanks in Dwayne's information. Her hands are trembling when she signs, and some pages get knocked to the floor. When the admitting clerk finally has what she needs, Jeannie comes with me to the chaplains' room, the only relatively quiet place in the trauma unit. A small couch, three chairs, a desk, a phone—everything in the room is beige, except for the phonebooks and Rayshawn, sitting on the couch, asleep. A young security officer has accompanied us from admitting, but in spite of my gestures, for some reason he does not remove Rayshawn. I don't have time to argue with him.

Jeannie's stunned eyes are wide but unseeing. In a shaky voice she asks to go to the chapel, her last-ditch strategy to make this awful nightmare disappear. I tell her I'll take her there as soon as the doctor has spoken with her. (Hospital protocol dictates that medical staff must deliver news of death; chaplains deal with the aftermath of that delivery.)

Jeannie has not yet been told the reason Dwayne is here, and she realizes she is being put off; fear of the worst overcomes her. She crumples into the desk chair, folds her arms onto the desk, and begins sobbing into them. I walk over, silently hold her shoulders, and encourage her tears.

The sound of her crying rouses Rayshawn from his stupor on the couch. He unfolds, gets up, muscles his way in between Jeannie and me. He stands behind Jeannie, drapes his body over hers, and presses his chin against her cheek. Making sexual movements with his whole body, he says, with each thrust, "It's all fucked up, man, it's all fucked up, it's all fucked up, it's all fucked up," a sickening mixture of rap and consolation and coitus.

I can't stand it, and put my hand on Rayshawn's arm to stop him. He whirls around and shouts, "Don't you touch me! And don't you touch her, neither!"

Unaccountably, the security officer has disappeared, and Rayshawn is between me and the door. I back off.

A doctor comes in to pronounce that Dwayne is dead. Jeannie's screams keep him from giving her any other information. I move to hold Jeannie. The doctor, assuming that Rayshawn is a brother, gives him the details of how Dwayne died: the bullet entered his left chest, went directly to the heart. There are also severe injuries to the head where Dwayne was probably pistol-whipped before he was shot.

Two policemen enter the room. They need Jeannie to officially identify her son. I assure her I'll go with her. Rayshawn says he's coming too, and though I whisper to the cops that this is not a good idea, they opt not to stop him. The cops lead the way. I support Jeannie, who is walking numbly. Behind us Rayshawn has begun chanting to himself, "Bad shit comin' down, man, bad shit comin' down," as a guard behind the counter presses a hidden button. Two metal doors swing open to allow us into the treatment area.

We file into the curtained cubicle where Dwayne lies. Jeannie touches his chest, then slumps to the floor, wailing. Blood has seeped through the clean sheets that cover his body. An emergency airway tube is still tied into his mouth. His young legs are long, and his feet hang over the edge of the gurney. The sight of running shoes at the ends of his dead legs makes my throat constrict. A nurse brings in a folding chair for Jeannie.

Rayshawn stands stunned at Dwayne's head, stroking his friend's hair nervously and saying, "Oh, man-n-n, oh, man-n-n."

The cops are motionless and quiet; they've seen this all before.

So have I. Yet for me each time is a first time. When it stops being the first time for me, it's time to quit.

Rayshawn looks at his right hand. There is blood on it. He studies it, frowning in confusion. Then, as if to confirm the reality of what lies before him, he returns his hand to his dead buddy's head and rests it there. Time stops. No one speaks. Jeannie is silent. No one moves. Everything is transfixed in a huge inheld breath.

At last Jeannie staggers up from her chair, starts out of

the cubicle, and says quietly, to nobody in particular, "Yes, that's my boy. That's Dwayne."

Jeannie and I return to the beige chaplains' room, where she will make phone calls, make decisions about her son's body, fill out required forms. Especially at times like these, I hate this room with its odd triangular shape (it was an afterthought in the emergency department planning), its over-whelmingly neutral color, and its lack of windows. One pathetic philodendron plant gasps for light and air on the desk beside me as I sit with Jeannie and coach her through the next steps in the paperwork.

Rayshawn comes and goes from the room in the restlessness of chemicals wearing off. He uses the beige phone to call his mother; his words have no coherence, and he is growing angry because she doesn't understand what he wants her to hear.

Alice, a friend of Jeannie's, arrives to be with her. We three talk quietly, until Rayshawn's voice, rising in anger at his mother, overrides ours. Although she is a stranger to him, Alice steps toward Rayshawn and takes the phone from him gently but firmly. He does not protest. Alice introduces herself into the phone and explains to Rayshawn's mother what has happened, tells her how hard this has been on Rayshawn. And the angry young man begins to cry. Alice holds him like a child with her free arm while she finishes the call and hangs up the phone. Then she quietly rocks him in both arms, crooning to him. Rayshawn melts down out of her arms onto the floor and sobs, great heaving, choking sounds.

Half an hour later Jeannie and Alice, Rayshawn and I return to the treatment cubicle to be with Dwayne's body one last time. Again Rayshawn cradles his friend's bloodied head,

this time more soberly. We stay for a while in silence, letting the violent reality of this death sink in.

When Jeannie is ready to leave, Alice holds the cubicle curtain aside for her. I follow. But I glance back just in time to witness a moment of profound liturgy.

In a precious fragment of time, Rayshawn is transformed from punk to priest. He stands at a gurney altar. He pulls his hand away from Dwayne's head, slowly. He studies his fingers in an attitude of prayer. Tears well up in his eyes. Then, in a reverent ritual of brotherhood and remembrance, Rayshawn deliberately licks the blood from his hand.

❧

Reflection Questions

1. For you, what is the most uncomfortable detail of this story? Did anything feel positive?

2. The police and hospital security ignored Rayshawn; the chaplain rejected him; Jeannie was helpless with him; Alice embraced him. How would you have responded to this complex young man?

3. What do you guess about Alice's life from this story? What qualities made her a good friend?

4. How can the author possibly call the final scene a "liturgy? Why is the story entitled "Eucharist" (Christian Communion, thanksgiving)?

ONE PIECE AT A TIME

*H*er whole house is brown—with aged dark cedar siding, mossy dark cedar roof shingles, peeling brown paint on gutters and trim, it's what some ironically call "Pacific Northwest chic."

Outside the windowed corner where Margaret regularly spends her days, three bird feeders hang at drunken angles, each empty except for a film of mildew. Once-treasured conch shells, spaced evenly along the deck's side railing, have become weathered gray traps in which spider webs catch moths and pine needles. English ivy has reclaimed the back steps and the wooden deck supports. Scores of cedars and Douglas firs loom behind and over everything, enclosing the dark and dank property, keeping out the sun.

As I ring the doorbell, a daddy longlegs crawls across the glass panes set into the front door. Raising each leg high, testing his footing as he goes, he picks his way across the door as an old woman's voice yells, "Come in," and my caregiving shift begins.

It is Friday morning, time for Margaret's once-a-week bath. Every Friday she sighs, "Do we have to?"

And every Friday I say, "Yes, but we'll do it really quickly, and then I'll fix lunch."

There is comfort for us both in the predictability of our script and of our routine. Every Friday I turn on the heater

in the bathroom and put the plastic bath bench into the tub. Every Friday I cover the bench with a small towel so her bare skin can slide across more easily. Every Friday I lay out two bath towels and pile her clean clothes on the counter in the order in which we'll need them: panties, bra, blouse, pants, one sock, one shoe.

After her bath I push Margaret's wheelchair to the corner of the living room where the two windows come together. She doesn't like to face the light because, she says, it hurts her eye. She has me back her into the corner, facing away from the light and the windows and the deck. The empty bird feeders and the scruffy seashells have long ago faded from her notice.

My favorite time with Margaret comes when she has finished her lunch. I take her dishes to the kitchen, turn off the TV, and get ready to massage her one and a half legs. The other half leg has been surgically removed, about six inches below the knee. "Diabetes," she explained. The skin of the stump has been folded over truncated muscle and bone like a neatly constructed pastry, decorated with scars.

She has also lost an eye ("My brother was swinging a golf club, and I was in the right place at the wrong time"), her appendix ("I don't know what they're for anyway"), a portion of her intestines ("They tell me there are plenty left in there, so I'm not worried much, except when they don't work so well"), and the tip of her left little finger ("I was clumsy in the kitchen").

"But sometimes," Margaret once said, "it does seem as if God's taking me from this world one piece at a time."

Margaret puts her arms tight around my neck and pulls herself up just a little so I can remove her slacks. I raise the

leg supports of her wheelchair and prop her leg and a half on pillows. She resettles with her lap covered by an afghan she crocheted fifty years ago. I sit on a footstool to the side of her left leg, the whole one. We always start with that one, so it can "teach" the other leg how to feel better. Today the nerves in the stub of her right leg are "acting up" and causing pain and a burning sensation, so the left leg has lots of teaching to do.

I spread massage lotion on my palms and place my hands just above her left knee. I hold them there for a few seconds while I watch Margaret breathe, and I coordinate my breathing with hers. Then I spread the lotion over her thigh, down to her knee, and down her calf to her ankle, foot, and toes. Long strokes back up the leg, and then ten minutes of gently encouraging her muscles to relax and release and renew. In the china cabinet on the far side of the room, an anniversary clock rotates its golden pendulum clockwise, counter-clockwise, clockwise, ticking its seconds into the sweet contented silence.

After I replace the afghan over Margaret's left leg, I repeat the same massage strokes on the amputated leg, including the long sweeps down the calf to the ankle, foot and toes, stroking what to my eyes seems to be empty space above the pillows. Back up to the thigh and then, her breath catching, Margaret suddenly directs me to move my hands to where the worst of her pain is, on the ball of her right foot. She points vaguely. "A little farther down, by the big toe," she says. My hands adjust, referring to her left foot as a gauge, massaging the shape of where the right foot once was but isn't any more, yet where pain is now.

Doctors call this "phantom limb" and "phantom pain," but for Margaret there is nothing unreal about it. For

Margaret her missing leg has shape, solidity, and location just as it did before the amputation, and pain registers in her brain as sharply as if the leg were still there. She has been given a prescription for the pain, but she says it makes her feel "wonky," and she doesn't like it. So every time I come, after her lunch we massage her "two" legs.

My eyes are half closed as I gently massage her stump. I am "seeing" with the tips of my fingers, searching through the scars for a sense of where my fingers are needed. Into our silence Margaret says, "Well, look at that," and my eyes refocus. A daddy longlegs has just hiked himself up onto her afghan. I know that this is a benevolent creature, but I am bemused that Margaret isn't disturbed by it. We both watch, fascinated as he maneuvers his way across the crocheted pattern, his eight delicate legs transporting his button body in a slow choreography of purpose. Eventually, he crawls down the other side, across the floor, and disappears behind a magazine rack.

To my surprise, Margaret begins to weep. My hands keep up their rhythmic motions, but I watch her face, and wait for her to speak. "I was so bad," she says, sniffling and blowing into a tissue. "When I was a little girl I used to torture them."

"Who?" I ask.

"The daddy longlegs. They were called 'harvestmen' where I came from. I'd catch one in my hand, then pull off one of those long thin legs. I'd watch the leg kick on my palm for a minute or two. When finally it stopped, I'd uncurl my hand, pull another leg off the poor creature, and be amused for another two minutes."

As she speaks, I remember too, though I'd be embarrassed to admit it aloud. I was four, I think, and I giggled

with each jerk of a severed spider leg. I find myself wondering, did Margaret's leg spasm when it was cut off? Do you suppose a daddy longlegs can have phantom pain?

Margaret's tears fall faster now. "Each time, at the end, there would be nothing left in my hand but a living spot with two terrified eyes. I'd just throw it away because it didn't interest me anymore." She stares past me, to a faraway time, remembering. After a long silence she says, "One day I finally realized what I was doing. I took a harvestman with three legs to my mother. I asked her if we could glue the other legs back on. My mother was gentle. She took the creature and its legs from me, and told me that the damage could not be undone. Then she held me while I sobbed."

And who was there to hold Margaret, I wonder, when God made all those decisions through the years to take her out of this world "one piece at a time"?

The clock in the cabinet ticks; my thumbs hold a place among her scars; Margaret's tears slow. "Ah," says Margaret, sighing, "right there, that's good." Her face relaxes as the phantom pain begins to recede, along with the painful memories. She blows her nose, and smiles tentatively.

Her dark home is now a refuge for daddy longlegs. Though I don't ask, I believe that in Margaret's mind this sanctuary is reparation for the harm she did to their eight-legged forebears seven decades ago. In her theology of fault and forgiveness, things seem to have balanced out: for the time being, Margaret is content to stay yet another day in what God has left her of her body.

❧

Reflection Questions

1. How do you respond to the concept of "phantom pain"?

2. Have you ever intentionally harmed, or even tortured, a living creature? How did it feel at the time? How do you feel about it now?

3. Is Margaret "philosophical" or "in denial" about losing so many parts of her body?

4. Describe the balance that Margaret has found between the past and the present.

THE SWEET SMELL OF URINE

I let myself into the house, tiptoe down the hallway, and peek into the dawn-dark room. My nose senses what my eyes will confirm as soon as I flip on the light: Noreen Frances woke up wet again today. The blankets, the sheets, the bed, her baby blue flannel pajamas with the silver stars on them, all are soaked with urine. Her disposable diaper fairly quivers from the strain of holding more than it was ever designed to absorb. She rubs her eyes and yawns broadly.

"Where did all that pee come from, Norrie?" I ask.

"Dunno," she says. Like a typical two-year-old, she expects me to have my own answers.

Norrie and I toddle into the bathroom. She stands beside her special toilet seat. While I kneel, wrestling with the sodden diaper now at her ankles, she pees on my hands—warm, yellow, totally unexpected pee. We stare at each other in astonishment; then we both laugh because, well . . . what else could we do?

After I clean and dry her and the floor and me, I help her pull on elastic-waist denim pants. Then, when I try to get her arms into her shirt, she keeps her elbows straight, won't look to see where the armholes are, doesn't want to help. With the putting on of her shoes she cooperates, chanting with me, "Toe in, heel down; good job, Noreen Frances!" When it

is time to put on her sweater she says, "Ow," the whole time.

Norrie says "ow" a lot, and by that she means "I hurt" and "I don't like that." Sometimes when she says "ow" she means "This juice tastes sour" or "Your hands are cold" or, often, "I don't want to." She has discovered that "ow" gets more attention than other words.

Norrie doesn't have a large vocabulary, yet sometimes she startles me with full sentences. Mostly, though, she says, "No," "Don't wanna," "Don't do that," and, with sur-prising authority, "That's enough!"

Noreen Frances has a strong will. When it flares, I try to remember that we have only a short time to be together. Too soon she won't need my care anymore, won't frustrate and delight me in the ways only she can. I try to see her through grandmother eyes; I wish for her to know what it feels like to be utterly cherished.

But I am not her grandmother. I am not even related to her. Yet I agonize over the changes that the next few hours hold for her.

She sits on a stool at the kitchen counter while I fix her favorite breakfast of scrambled eggs and ketchup and toast. She eats most of it with her fingers, and gets ketchup on her nose.

Then the two men arrive. Their shoulders are tense, their smiles false. They hug and kiss Noreen Frances. Norrie says, "Ow," and wets her pants. After I have gotten her dry and dressed again, the two men stand on either side of her and guide her toward the door. They have gathered up a few bags of her belongings, and they take her away, to live in another place: more safe, more sterile, with others more like her.

For Norrie isn't two years old. She is eighty-four. Alzheimer's disease has claimed all of her brain except for a

toddler's allotment of memories and words; it has left her a little bit of curiosity, a lot of fear, some delight, and her tenacious will.

Ten years of the disease have erased the stunt pilot, the air traffic controller, the wife, the mother, the dog breeder and trainer; they have taken away the fisherwoman, the seamstress, the tennis champ, and even the loving grandmother. The disease has left her with no way to understand who she is, or where she is, or what is happening to her. Alzheimer's has stolen from her elder's body all but a child's chunk of mind, and left none of a child's potential.

So those two men, the strangers who are her sons, escort her out into the morning, away from her home. "Ow!" she yells from the sidewalk, confused and afraid. "No!" she says, and resists them with all her considerable strength and her rigid arms. "Ow," she wails, as they bend her stiffened body into the back seat of a car and fasten the seat belt around her. "Ow," I hear, faintly, as they drive off.

I lock the front door of Norrie's house and walk to my car. For several minutes hot tears slide down the steering wheel where I lay my head. Eventually there is nothing left to do but blow my nose, shout, "Ow!" over and over again, and reluctantly drive away.

Half an hour later I awaken ninety-year-old Vera. She, too, lies in urine-soaked sheets and blankets. She is perplexed and angry: Where the hell has all that chilly wetness come from?

Sometimes I am tempted to tell her. I want her to take the blame for the mess, because she refuses to wear diapers at night. But I hold my tongue, coax her out of bed, and guide her wobbly steps to the bathroom.

After she sheds her soggy robe, she stands there, nakedly wondering what to do next. She certainly is not going to take a shower, no way! In the tub after a protracted discussion, she whines and grouses and tries to escape while I struggle to clean her fragile skin with water that she says is too cold . . . too hot . . . too cold, and soap that slips and "stinks."

Once out of the tub, however, we begin the best part of her morning ritual: getting ready to "meet her date for breakfast." We giggle together as she looks into the mirror, combs her hair, and puts on lipstick, all the while talking about "my guy." When she is ready, I turn her over to Raymond, her husband of more than sixty years.

Once again, as he does every morning, "her guy" greets her as if she is the most beautiful girl in the world. He positions her chair for her at the table. He pours the milk into her bowl of cornflakes and doles out her morning pills. He fills their cups with the strong black coffee that bolsters both of them all day long. For half an hour they will be on their breakfast date. Then they'll move to the glassed-in porch, to soak up the sun and to nap.

Vera's bedroom is filled with books she can no longer read, mementos of her Scandinavian childhood, and certificates of her achievements as a nurse, surgical assistant, and hospital administrator. In the middle of it all is Vera's bed, with a swamp of cold urine retained in the depression of a clear plastic mattress protector. If she were still able, she'd efficiently clean and sanitize and make that bed ready again for its patient; if she knew who the patient was, whose urine it was, she'd be mortified.

Hers is another brain ravaged by Alzheimer's disease. At first, when the disease was new to her, she made labels to

help her recognize things from one moment to the next. There are little pieces of paper still taped around the house, reminding her that these are "plastic bags" or this is a "coffee cup" or "unopened oatmeal" or something "empty." One sad note taped to a doorframe asks, "What is this?" She cannot recognize her once-beloved old dog, yet she can still sing the Norwegian national anthem.

As I bundle up the soaked linens and carry them to the utility room, a cloud of eye-watering ammonia surrounds me.

But on this day, for some reason I do not recoil. Maybe Noreen Frances would understand why. Maybe Vera understands.

Whatever the reason, on this day I surrender, letting the fumes permeate my being. The pungent smell of urine—a scent that in our culture is not okay; an odor that must be masked, apologized for, cleared away immediately—becomes blessed, and for a brief moment I understand that in our fragile, ammonia-scented, question-soaked human lives, Vera and I, and Noreen Frances too, are one.

As I close the washing machine lid, I am almost sad to lose the gift of that holy incense.

∽

Reflection Questions

1. How is care of a two-year-old different from care of an eighty-four-year old with dementia?

2. How would you know what Norrie meant by "Ow"?

3. What frightens you most when you think about Alzheimer's disease?

4. Do you see meaning and purpose in the current lives of Norrie and Vera?

MACK THE HERMIT

*I*n the last two months Mack has been too weak to refuse help any longer. He is no less strong-willed, but he chooses to direct his strength and his will inward. He seems no longer to care whether his tiny space is invaded, so long as his silence is maintained. Mack is not mean-spirited; it is simply his choice to be a hermit. The written word— others' and his own—is his preferred company. Words of poetry and classic literature fill his mind and his space. He cherishes silence broken only by fine music and the birds outside his shack that seem to sing just for him.

What I know about Mack is a mélange of local legend swirled into the intimate physicality of tending his dying body, and sweetened by his profound silence. Before his final illness Mack admitted only a select few into his life: Ted has known him for forty years, and Ted's wife, Louise, has known Mack almost as long. But for most of the folks who live on Whidbey Island, "Whiskey Mack" is a shadowy figure who occasionally hiked to town for supplies and sometimes did odd jobs for cash. Otherwise he kept to himself. He lived in a tiny, handcrafted aerie that he built above a beach on the southern tip of the island; it was accessible only by a cliff-side rope ladder. There he wrote plays, novels, and poetry on a manual typewriter. He used to make his living as a manuscript typist; reputedly he could type 120 words a minute with no errors.

When, after ten years, his original shack succumbed to a mudslide, Mack moved down to the beach and built himself another house out of found materials: used lumber, discarded windows, linoleum remnants. Fourteen turquoise-colored shutters, salvaged from somewhere, created the windbreak that became his back porch.

The house that Mack built is nestled in madrona trees filled with songbirds and seabirds and hawks and owls. It is big enough inside for a twenty-four-inch-wide chair to fit between a twenty-four-inch-wide cot and an eighteen-inch-deep counter that serves as table and desk, and still have room for a person to walk between the chair and the counter—if that person turns sideways. And from floor to ceiling, every wall sprouts the shelves that hold Mack's beloved books: half a dozen translations of Homer's works, a whole spectrum of classical writers, all the plays of Shakespeare, a wealth of poetry and commentary, and enough unabridged and specialty dictionaries to make a reference librarian swoon. Row after row of books insulates, protects, and reflects Mack's life.

At age sixty-three, five decades of smoking have caught up with him, and Mack has developed lung cancer. Ted saw that Mack got to medical appointments, but when the medical options were exhausted, Ted began to come daily to Mack's place to tend to him. And when Ted could no longer do all that needed to be done, a rota of caregivers was set up. Each of us who volunteered was vetted by Mack in an hour of silence in his very small space; after that "interview," Mack would nod yes or no to indicate whether or not the candidate was accepted.

There is no plumbing in his house and no electrical

service. A very long water hose and an equally long extension cord run down the beach, connecting Mack's place to the nearest summer cottage. Whether or not the neighbors are aware of their donation, those of us who care for Mack are very grateful, especially for the water.

Usually Mack sits in his chair all day, which leaves just a corner of his cot for a caregiver to sit on. There are the back steps, too, but that requires an awkward coming in again, from behind Mack's chair, and breaking into the space and the silence in order to check on him. On my first day, sitting on the edge of the cot, I tried initiating conversation. That went nowhere with Mack. The intensity of his eyes, although kind, nevertheless discouraged talk—his remaining time was too short to fill with talk that could never be adequate for this experience. Once I tried taking a book to read, but the weight of Mack's silence shouted for attentiveness. This is not a time to be distracted by words, either spoken or written. This is a time to witness the mortality of potential, to grieve the too-young dying of a brother, to ponder my own body's cells expiring by the thousands even as I sit with Mack.

This sitting in silence has a feet-to-the-flame quality that is terrible at the same time that it is pure gift. No Zen master could call forth from me more than Mack's mortal silence does. And no spiritual exercise could demand of me more humility than the changing of Mack's diaper. We have worked out a routine in which he puts his arms around my neck so I can help him to stand. His full gray beard gets in my way, and I can't see at all until he is vertical enough to let go of my neck and reach for the wooden crossbeam just above me. He holds on to that while I quickly pull down his sweat pants, unfasten the diaper, and remove it. I clean his skin

with baby wipes or a washcloth, dry him quickly, and put a fresh disposable diaper between his legs. This process is not as easy with an upright six-foot tall man as it is with a baby on a changing table! By now his legs are wobbling from the effort of standing, and I might or might not get the fastener tapes in the right places. But Mack is patient with my fumbling, and as quickly as possible he is back in his chair, with one blanket over his lap and another around his shoulders.

As Mack becomes weaker and his breathing more difficult, Ted contacts Enso House, a residential hospice connected with the Zen monastery several miles away. Mack agrees to move; one afternoon the monks carry him from his hermitage and transport him to the hospice. There he will have the luxury of a warm shower and a clean bed. There he will be quietly attended around the clock and kept pain-free.

A few afternoons later I stop at Enso House to say goodbye to Mack. He is not eating or drinking anymore, so it won't be long before he dies. The monk who is at his side rises to leave me alone with Mack. I hold Mack's hand, look into his huge brown eyes, which seem even larger now with his face shrunken behind his long beard. I thank Mack for his creativity, for his integrity, and for what he has taught me about the richness of silence. I tell him how honored I am to have been allowed into his dying time. Then I kiss his hand and stand to leave.

But Mack won't let go of my hand.

I sit back down and lay my forehead against our joined hands.

Suddenly, I feel as if my heart has burst open. Words come spilling out of my mouth, words of love and fear, of

grief and confusion, words I did not know were waiting to be spoken, words I did not know I even knew. All of those words incubated in Mack's silence. Into his welcoming presence all my words now flow.

Then, just as unexpectedly, the words are finished and the silence that follows is crystalline, like the air after a sudden rain. Mack releases my hand. I kiss him on the forehead and wish him a good journey to whatever comes after life.

Mack dies the next morning, calmly and with great dignity, true to himself—deep in his chosen silence to the end.

❧

Reflection Questions

1. Would you be able to pass Mack's "sitting in silence" test? Why, or why not?

2. What might have happened if Mack had not agreed to move to the residential hospice?

3. What do you feel you could offer Mack, sitting at his bedside?

4. What gifts did Mack have to offer in his silent dying?

EPILOGUE

It's Reciprocal

*I*n the center of the fifteenth row of a large auditorium, I wait in the dark for the Saratoga Orchestra to begin their concert. The conductor has taken his place on the podium; he makes eye contact with the musicians, raises his hands. He scoops up the first notes of Mendelssohn's *Hebrides Overture* and pulls the sounds out and over the audience.

And I realize that I am weeping. It is not because of the music, lovely and emotional though that is. My tears are, instead, a sudden recognition of what really happened earlier today.

This morning I spoke at a local church about the book —this book—that had been "writing me" for the past several years. I read the words of the prologue, Gloria's story. I then challenged the congregation with the questions and the gifts I have gathered from the margins. This morning was the first public presentation of the manuscript on its way to being published.

I weep in the darkened auditorium now for the joy of having done as I was asked. All along, my unspoken instructions from the people of the margins have been to *dare . . . see . . . be present . . . return . . . say.*

The single essential skill for being in the margins is presence. I had to *dare* to step into the margins, but this

alone was not enough. Not till I had let the people of the margins define themselves could I *see* them. Not till I could see them could I *be present* to them. Not till I was willing to *return* with this knowledge to my own world at the center and *say* what I had learned in the margins was I able to complete the sacred task I'd been given—to share the wisdom of the margins with the larger world.

We all inhabit some margin, if only in our own hidden opinions of ourselves—and sometimes only in the dying days of our own lives. My prayer for each of us is that we dare to recognize and enter these personal margins with deep compassion for ourselves and for one another.

Now the music swells around me, my tears abate, and I am warmed by a compassionate understanding that though I continue to go to the margins of our culture, it is never easy. After all these years I am still challenged, still out of my comfort zone, still tempted to retreat, no matter which margin I approach.

Every day, every time I stand at the threshold to a margin, I hear the mantra of its instructions, like the rhythms that fill this auditorium: *dare . . . see . . . be present . . . return . . . say.*

And always, always, always there is the tone of Gloria's husky voice reaching out to me across that threshold, reiterating: *It's reciprocal.*

About the Author

photo credit: Chris Mann, PhD

CYNTHIA TRENSHAW earned national certification as hospital chaplain and as massage therapist. She holds WA state certifications as professional guardian, guardian ad litem, and nursing assistant-registered. She holds a master's degree in theology (MTh) from Jesuit School of Theology at Berkeley. Three of the chapters from *Meeting in the Margins* have been published in an anthology and a literary journal, and her essays and poetry have been published in a variety of magazines and journals over the past ten years. She blogs regularly at www.cynthiatrenshaw.com.

100 Under $100: One Hundred Tools for Empowering Global Women by Betsy Teutsch. $29.95, 978-1-63152-934-4. An inspiring, comprehensive look at the many tools being employed today to empower women in the developing world and help them raise themselves out of poverty.

Renewable: One Woman's Search for Simplicity, Faithfulness, and Hope by Eileen Flanagan. $16.95, 978-1-63152-968-9. At age forty-nine, Eileen Flanagan had an aching feeling that she wasn't living up to her youthful ideals or potential, so she started trying to change the world and in doing so, she found the courage to change her life.

Don't Leave Yet: How My Mother's Alzheimer's Opened My Heart by Constance Hanstedt. $16.95, 978-1-63152-952-8. The chronicle of Hanstedt's journey toward independence, self-assurance, and connectedness as she cares for her mother, who is rapidly losing her own identity to the early stage of Alzheimer's.

A Leg to Stand On: An Amputee's Walk into Motherhood by Colleen Haggerty. $16.95, 978-1-63152-923-8. Haggerty's candid story of how she overcame the pain of losing a leg at seventeen and of terminating two pregnancies as a young woman and went on to become a mother, despite her fears.

Where Have I Been All My Life? A Journey Toward Love and Wholeness by Cheryl Rice. $16.95, 978-1-63152-917-7. Rice's universally relatable story of how her mother's sudden death launched her on a journey into the deepest parts of grief and, ultimately, toward love and wholeness.

The Great Healthy Yard Project: Our Yards, Our Children, Our Responsibility by Diane Lewis, MD. $24.95, 978-1-938314-86-5. A comprehensive look at the ways in which we are polluting our drinking water and how it's putting our children's future at risk and what we can do to turn things around.

CPSIA information can be obtained at www.ICGtesting.com
Printed in the USA
LVOW11s0624090915

453393LV00002B/2/P

9 781631 528163